Tea with Edie and Fitz

By Adam Pasen

Tea With Edie and Fitz (1st ed. 2015)
Copyright © 2015 Adam Pasen

Produced by special arrangement with
CHICAGO DRAMAWORKS of Chicago, IL
www.ChicagoDramaworks.com

To Edith, Scott, Zelda, and Henry - for
your stories both written and lived -
and also to my mother, Launa.

Acknowledgements

Tea with Edie and Fitz received its first working production in York Arena Theatre on the campus of Western Michigan University in July of 2011. The production was directed by D. Terry Williams, stage managed by Brad Van Houten, with scenic design by Kyle Moore, costumes by Kate MacKenzie and hair/wigs by Garrylee McCormick. The cast was as follows:

F. Scott Fitzgerald	Christopher Grazul
Zelda Fitzgerald	Susie Parr
Edith Wharton	Elizabeth Terrel
Henry James	G. William Zorn
Photographer/Chanler/Wharton/ Scribner/Perkins/Campbell	Mitch Voss
Grossie/Secretary	Chelsea Morgan

Tea with Edie and Fitz received its professional world premiere in May 2013 at the Greenhouse Theatre in Chicago with the Dead Writers Theatre Collective. The production was directed by Jim Schneider, stage managed by Matthew Bonaccorso, assistant directed by Reed Motz, with scenic design by Edward Matthew Walter, costumes by Elizabeth Wislar, props by Jeffrey Shields, lighting by Linda Bulgieski, sound by Jeffrey Levin, and dramaturgy by Katherine Joslin and Aaron Henrickson. The cast was as follows:

F. Scott Fitzgerald	Madison Niederhauser
Zelda Fitzgerald	Nora Lise Ulrey
Edith Wharton	Patti Roeder
Henry James	Michael Graham
Chanler	Nelson Rodriguez
Photographer	Brandon Johnson
Grossie	Christina Irwin
Wharton	Peter Esposito
Scribner	Bill Chamberlain
Secretary	Megan Delay
Perkins	Luke Renn
Campbell	Ben Muller
Understudies	Brandon Johnson
	Tracey Green
	G. William Zorn

All productions of this play are required to include the following credit on the title page of the program:
Tea with Edie and Fitz received its professional world premiere with the Dead Writers Theatre Collective in May of 2013.

Setting
Post WWI France in the roaring twenties, bursting with famous literary expatriates. The Paris flat of Zelda and Scott Fitzgerald and the sprawling French estate of Edith Wharton at Colombe, with a quick detour to the publishing offices of Charles Scribner in New York. Scenes shift forward and backward in time before and after the legendary meeting of Edith and Scott at Pavillon Colombe. Scott's scenes start at the end chronologically and move backwards, Edith's start at the beginning chronologically and move forward. The scenes cross in the middle in Charles Scribner's office.

Cast of Characters
FITZGERALD - author of *The Great Gatsby*. Late 20's.
ZELDA - his Southern wife. Late 20's.
EDITH - author of *The Age of Innocence*. 60's.
GHOST OF JAMES - Henry James, Edith's mentor and companion, author of *The Golden Bowl*. 60's - or can appear as he did earlier in their acquaintance.
PHOTOGRAPHER
GROSSIE - Edith Wharton's longtime governess and confidante.
SCRIBNER - iconic New York publisher at the turn of the century.
SECRETARY
PERKINS - Fitzgerald's agent at Scribner's.
WHARTON - Edith's mentally disturbed ex-husband.
CAMPBELL - Fitzgeralds' frequent visitor in France.
CHANLER - Quiet mutual acquaintance of Edith and Fitzgerald.

The play is meant to be performed with 6 actors (3M, 3F) with one man as PHOTOGRAPHER/ SCRIBNER/ PERKINS/ WHARTON/ CAMPBELL/ CHANLER, and one woman as GROSSIE/ SECRETARY. The roles can also be broken up. All in all the play calls for 6-12 actors.

Tea with Edie and Fitz

By Adam Pasen

SCENE ONE

The Fitzgeralds' Paris Flat.
A room overflowing with paintings. They lean against every
wall, overlapping each other. Jazz plays from the record
player on the floor: "Ain't We Got Fun?" ZELDA sits at a
canvas at the center of the room contemplating her next
brush stroke. She is wearing a full tutu. FITZGERALD
enters.

FITZGERALD
She beat me!

ZELDA
re: the painting
Scott, look...it's pretty good, isn't it? Yes, I really think
there's something here -

FITZGERALD
Turning music down
Did you hear what I said? She beat me!

ZELDA
I heard you. Well, what did you expect? To get along
famously?

FITZGERALD
I don't...that's not the...

Pause.

FITZGERALD
She BEAT ME!

ZELDA
Does this seem too deco to you? Because I'd really like to try something new with this one. Cubist...or surrealist. Oh, I am simply mad for the surrealists, you know!

Beat. She sighs, turns from the painting.

I assume you don't mean she beat you literally. She's probably corseted too tight to make a fist without fainting.

FITZGERALD
Would you be more inclined to listen if I said she did?

ZELDA
Well, it would be novel...ironically more so than any of her novels. I guess I would.

FITZGERALD
Yes! Literally struck me! Nearly gave me a black ey -

Zelda lowers the paintbrush a notch.

Well, at any rate she was a near virago, I tell you.

Beat. Zelda spins in her seat.

ZELDA
All right, I'll bite. Fisticuffs get me every time. Tell me all about how literary titans Edith Wharton and F. Scott Fitzgerald faced off over...tea, was it?

FITZGERALD
Earl Grey, no less. Oh, how it's seared into my memory, like it were yesterday -

ZELDA
It was a few hours ago -

FITZGERALD
Just like it were yesterday...the Jazz Age and the Gilded Age duking it out once and for all...it would make quite the movie, maybe I can do the title cards -

ZELDA
Out with it!

FITZGERALD
All right! Well, as you know, when she found out I was a fellow expat in Paris the great Grand Dame invited me to the Pavillon Colombe, and I brought Teddy along. You know Teddy - Teddy Chanler? Those depressive musician types can always use a day out in the sun. Of course that wasn't exactly what we had in store...

Lights shift and flicker over the stage and the sound of a projector plays. The scene is played by actors as a silent film.

FITZGERALD and CHANLER approach and knock. EDITH answers. FITZGERALD salutes warmly and offers his hand.

Title card: "Mrs. Wharton, what an honor."

EDITH bows with painful duration and formality.

Title card: "You may enter." The three seat themselves.

*FITZGERALD and EDITH on either side with CHANLER in
the middle. Long painful beat.*

Title card: "..."

FITZGERALD motions to a nearby vase.

Title card: "My, what a lovely vase."

Edith nods.

Title card: "Yes." Beat. Title card: "Tea?"

*FITZGERALD goes through a series of enthusiastic gestures
and a long and visibly emphatic speech of thanks that goes
on for several beats. When it is finally over...*

Title card: "Please."

*The three take tea. FITZGERALD motions to EDITH. Title
card: "Mrs. Wharton, I have an interesting story."*

*EDITH motions. Title card: "By all means, though I trust it
is not too vulgar."*

FITZGERALD acts the story out.

*Title card: "It is of a couple who arrive in France and must
seek temporary lodgings, finding a lovely little room that is
quite reasonable."*

*Title card: "They find the building populated by many lovely
and friendly young ladies."*

*Title card: "Finally, as they leave in the morning, a bystander
asks if they know they are staying at a house of ill-repute!"*

FITZGERALD laughs. Beat. Edith gestures.

Title card: "Mr. Fitzgerald, your story was heavy on exposition, rushed in the denouement, and forced in the climax. Take that!"

EDITH strikes FITZGERALD with her fan. FITZGERALD rises and pushes his chair back.

Title card: "I'm sorry, but I make it a point never to be beaten before 5:00 p.m. Excuse me."

FITZGERALD exits. EDITH rises huffily. Title card: "I never!"

EDITH exits. CHANLER is alone. He looks after FITZGERALD. He looks after EDITH. He looks forward. Beat. CHANLER shrugs and sips his tea. Sneezes.

Title card: "Ah-choo!"

The scene returns to the bedroom. ZELDA is doubled over with laughter.

ZELDA
She didn't!

FITZGERALD
Which part?

ZELDA
Analyze your anecdote..."forced in the climax?" I'll never believe it...

FITZGERALD
Practically verbatim.

ZELDA
Oh! And that poor Airedale Teddy, just sitting there leaking pathos all over the scene...I can just see it!

FITZGERALD
Interesting type, Teddy. He's the model for Francis Melarkey in my new novel.

ZELDA
Oh, Scott, you mustn't. Such a beautiful title, *Tender is the Night*, and such a hideously named protagonist.

FITZGERALD
What would be a better name?

ZELDA
Anything! Anything would be better! You could call him...Dick...Diver...

FITZGERALD
Dick Diver?

ZELDA
Yes...yes! You could call him Dick Diver and it would be a sounder choice! Not that I actually expect you to go through with it, of course...

Beat.

FITZGERALD
Why wouldn't I?

ZELDA
Well, the Scott I married would, but this mellow facsimile who has tea with Edith Wharton and waxes sympathetic

ZELDA
Continued
over milksops like Teddy Chanler...I don't think he's got it
in him.

FITZGERALD
I could do it.

ZELDA
Sure you could.

FITZGERALD
You don't believe me?

ZELDA
I don't kno-ow...

FITZGERALD
I'll do it! I'll call him Dick Diver, don't think I won't!

ZELDA
Dick Diver! And name him...Dick...Diver...

ZELDA bursts into peals of laughter.

FITZGERALD
Turning away
You don't have to mock me, Zelda.

*ZELDA'S laughter slows, then stops. She suddenly goes
vacant and stares emptily. FITZGERALD turns.*

Zelda?

Goes to her, kneeling.

FITZGERALD
Zelda?

ZELDA
I'm fine. I just...I just...

Beat. She pops up.

I want to go roller skating!

FITZGERALD
Roller skating?

ZELDA
Yes! Roller skating! On top of the Arc de Triomphe...look, I can see it right from the window!

ZELDA runs to the window

ZELDA
No wait...under the Eiffel Tower! Shock the baguettes right out of those Parisians' mitts!

FITZGERALD
I don't know if...

ZELDA
How do you expect to ever name your hero Dick Diver if a little thing like roller skating has you tied up in knots?

FITZGERALD
You're right. Let's go roller skating.

ZELDA
Don't be ridiculous. I can't go roller skating, I'm wearing a tutu.

FITZGERALD
I hadn't noticed.

ZELDA
It was in the trunk with the rest of my old clothes. It's the only one that didn't get ruined when I –

FITZGERALD
Zelda.

Beat.

ZELDA
Recognize it? The black with gold lace? From the first picture I ever sent you from Montgomery when you went home to St. Paul?

FITZGERALD
Of course I do.

ZELDA
It even still has the little danglers I sewed on it. See? I'm recapturing my youth.

ZELDA stand and shakes, the bells attached to the skirt jingling merrily.

I'm a Southern "bell," get it?

FITZGERALD
You're my Southern belle.

ZELDA
Am I "For Whom Your Bell Tolls?"

FITZGERALD
Yes.

ZELDA
Isn't that what Ernest said? What your great friend wants to
call his next masterpiece?

FITZGERALD
Zelda.

FITZGERALD goes to her and holds her. Beat.

ZELDA
All right. So I'm a bell then. But I'm more than that too,
Scott. I'm going to be an artist.

FITZGERALD
Wonderful, just so long as you don't get paint all over the
walls...this is the third hotel we've lived in this year, I'd like
to unpack at least before we get the boot.

ZELDA
Oh, I hate a room without an open suitcase...it seems so
permanent! Why, there's always more hotel rooms, more
money, and more booze - it's the Boom, Scott! Times of
plenty! But I don't care about material things, I just want to
live! Be a painter for starters.

FITZGERALD
Of course, and you know I think some of these are actually
quite good. You show promise without a doubt.

ZELDA
I'm going to be a ballerina too.

FITZGERALD
Well, it may be a little late to be a professional, but at twenty-five you could still achieve some distinction in your craft, maybe even teach...

ZELDA
Egorova has agreed to coach me privately. She didn't mind that I was late to our lunch at all. If all goes well, she wants to invite me into the Ballet Russe.

ZELDA does a combination across the floor.

FITZGERALD
I...that's...

ZELDA
Incredible? Unlikely? I agree! But it's true! And look...
She pulls her collar aside.

ZELDA
See the skin? All clear - I'm better! Because I have purpose again. Oh, I'm going to paint Scott!

FITZGERALD
Grand!

ZELDA
And I'm going to dance!

FITZGERALD
Wonderful!

ZELDA
And Scott...I'm going to write.

FITZGERALD stops smiling. END OF SCENE.

SCENE TWO

Pavillon Colombe. EDITH sitting austere and rigid in a chair. Long beat. A flashbulb goes off. EDITH exhales in relief and slumps in her chair as PHOTOGRAPHER moves onstage, fiddling with a camera.

PHOTOGRAPHER
Got it, Mrs. Wharton. You can relax.

EDITH
Too late, I'm afraid - Grossie! Gro...ah!

GROSSIE enters with dogs.

EDITH
Come, come here babies...

EDITH takes the dogs.

GROSSIE
They've been whining for you all morning Edie.

EDITH
Yes, dears, momma missed you...you know Grossie, you can say what you want about the larger breeds, but some day I believe that every young lady is going to carry a tiny toy dog with her, perhaps in her satchel, and she will take it everywhere with her and it will be a sign of good breeding and intelligence... *(to dogs)* Yes it will...yezzitwill...

GROSSIE
That's all very good miss, but now it's time for their bath -

PHOTOGRAPHER
All set, Mrs. Wharton.

EDITH
In a moment - Grossie, come, I want one with the dogs, like
I took after Teddy and I...well don't just stand there!

GROSSIE
Oh, Edie, not on your new brocade!

EDITH
Don't I pay people to clean my brocade?

GROSSIE
Oh, I don't think -

EDITH
Overlapping
Now come here and -

PHOTOGRAPHER
Shall I come back later?

EDITH AND GROSSIE
Stay put.

*PHOTOGRAPHER freezes. Beat. GROSSIE sighs and helps
EDITH place the dogs on her shoulders. GROSSIE backs
away. The flashbulb goes off. EDITH laughs and plays with
the dogs. She turns to PHOTOGRAPHER. Beat.*

EDITH
You are excused.

*PHOTOGRAPHER exits. GROSSIE comes and takes the
dogs.*

GROSSIE
Edie...just as I said! Little paw prints all over the collar...

EDITH
I imagine I can afford a new dress, if I must.

GROSSIE
But can you afford a new Catherine Gross when I keel over
from exhaustion?

EDITH
What a shame you never had the inclination to write,
Grossie...with such a flair for drama you would outsell me
in a fortnight.

GROSSIE
As you can see, miss...I've got my hands full. Ah! And while
I'm on the subject...

*GROSSIE jostles the dogs to one side and pulls a package
out of her apron.*

This came for you by the post today.

EDITH takes the package.

EDITH
From whom?

GROSSIE
Comes from New York. Scribners.

EDITH
Scribners. Ah. It must be the new proofs.

She opens the wrapping.

EDITH
I was nearly apoplectic over the last...no surprises this time
- I told Charles simple binding, no gilt or unnecessary
etchings, and a good strong fabric, green maybe...I...

EDITH stares at the book. Beat.

GROSSIE
What? What is it?

EDITH
I cannot say...it is not mine. *The Great Gatsby.*

EDITH reads the note.

EDITH
"Edith - the latest by a very promising young writer...much
obliged if...give a read...anxiously awaits your
thoughts...Charles Scribner."

GROSSIE
Do you know the writer?

EDITH
What is there to know? These new writers are all alike...he
is probably just writing to fill the lull between divorces.

GROSSIE
Well if any woman should be understanding on the topic of
divorce, miss, I would think it would be you.

EDITH
Yes, as a solemn possibility, not a casual diversion...now it
is practically de riguer -

GROSSIE
Under her breath
"By F. Scott Fitzgerald."

EDITH
Wait...Fitzgerald? Scott Fitzgerald, did you say?

EDITH takes the book from GROSSIE.

GROSSIE
You do know him...

EDITH
Peripherally...and that is more than enough. I seem to recall a sketch he wrote for College Humor about a group of stories conversing, and the Edith Wharton Story sits alone and glares haughtily until someone tells her that "her climax is on crooked."

Pause.

GROSSIE
That's not bad...

EDITH
Grossie!

GROSSIE
Well, what's wrong with a little send-up is all I ask? Half your novels are flat parody of Henry James!

EDITH
Homage, Grossie. Which I handled with delicacy and taste and which he very much appreciated.

GROSSIE
Appreciated? What was it he said about your piece for the Revue? That he "congratulates you on the way you've managed to pick up every old worn-out phrase that's been lying about the streets of Paris for the last twenty years and pack them into a few short pages?"

EDITH
Laughing
Wicked, wicked man! I find it hard to believe it has been almost a decade since...

Beat.

EDITH
At any rate, Grossie, thank you for bringing this in. If you care to return this afternoon, you can tend to it in the library, where it will most likely be accruing dust.

GROSSIE
Aren't you going to even give it a look?

EDITH
Give it a look? Why should I? I know what is in it! Drinking and extramarital relations, women wearing pants and...voting.

EDITH drops the book.

Besides, I wanted to continue my work on my memoir.

Pause. GROSSIE waits. EDITH turns to her expectantly.

GROSSIE
Of course, miss. Just ring if you need anything.

EDITH
Oh, and Grossie...I am 63 years old. Do you still think it
necessary to call me "miss?"

GROSSIE
You'll always be "miss" to me, miss.

*GROSSIE exits. EDITH sits at her desk, where a manuscript
is placed. She puts a leaf of paper in the typewriter and
begins to type. Beat. The GHOST OF JAMES appears, glass
of claret in hand. Looking dapper.*

GHOST OF JAMES
That was not all I said, you know.

EDITH
Not looking up
About what, Henry?

GHOST OF JAMES
About your story in the Revue des Deux Mondes. I was not
entirely critical after all.

EDITH
Oh?

GHOST OF JAMES
Yes, if you will recall, I told Walter later that evening that it
was "a very credible episode in your career..."

GHOST OF JAMES AND EDITH
But she must never do it again.

EDITH turns and smiles.

EDITH
Always honest, to the last painful letter.

GHOST OF JAMES
I had to be. It was the only way to console myself that you were selling so much better than I.

EDITH
You were merely stern, as a mentor should be. These young writers today want to skip the most precious phase of all - the seeking of approval! You and I never felt the need to puff one another, why toward the end I hardly remember discussing our work at all.

GHOST OF JAMES
There was no need. I knew how greatly you admired my later experiments in form.

EDITH
Evasive
Mmm.

Beat. GHOST OF JAMES looks at EDITH'S manuscript.

GHOST OF JAMES
Is that to be your latest best-seller, then? What shall it be called?

EDITH
A Backward Glance. My memoir. As you well know.

GHOST OF JAMES
Ah, of course, of course. Aptly named.

EDITH
And just what does that mean?

GHOST OF JAMES
My dear, you have reached your reflective phase.

EDITH
I beg your pardon?

GHOST OF JAMES
You are looking to the past, moving in reverse. It's the first step toward death.

EDITH
That is simply not true! Why, just yesterday I booked myself on an Aegean Cruise, just like the one I took as a girl...

GHOST OF JAMES
Quite the same! Recapturing is not living, Edith. You were happy on a boat once, so you do it again, now. But when we are young we sail on our youth. Now you will simply be an old woman, surrounded by fish -

EDITH
Walter is coming to visit.

Beat.

GHOST OF JAMES
He -

EDITH
Yes.

GHOST OF JAMES
And Edward?

EDITH
Teddy is still in Switzerland taking the cure for
his...nervousness. He shall be absent. Not that he was ever
particularly present as a husband. It's simply more...official
now.

GHOST OF JAMES
And you and Walter can pick up right where you left off -
when did you see him last?

EDITH
Not since the War. I brought him on my trip through France
to survey the devastation at the front. You remember - Le
Rire did that cartoon of us "Dans le Ruins," with Walter
looking bored and me surveying the destruction casually
through my lorgnette drawling "ce n'est que ca!"

GHOST OF JAMES
Mmm, "is that all..."

Beat.

I wasn't just translating, is there more to that story?

EDITH
Well, I suppose I should have resented the portrayal as a
coldhearted stoic, but when I saw myself in the cartoon, all I
could think was..."My God, am I that fat?"

Beat.

A woman should never grow stout, Henry. It is the body's
first betrayal. A girl thinks herself immune to time's
ravages. When she thickens, that first buttress crumbles and
she glimpses the abyss. To grow stout is a preview of death.

Pause.

GHOST OF JAMES
Well that seems a bit extreme, does it not? Besides, if anything is a preview of death it is this claret...

He drains the glass.

Terrible!

GHOST OF JAMES pours himself another glass and rises.

Well, Walter Berry coming here! That is something. Ah, well, I shan't dwell on it too much, you know how over-stimulation brings my stammer back on...

He begins to exit. EDITH turns.

EDITH
Where are you going?

GHOST OF JAMES
To ponder. To mull. Perhaps to frighten Grossie - "ghost things," you know. In the meantime, perhaps you should set your memoir aside and give that novel a perfunctory glass. It may help with Walter.

EDITH
How?

GHOST OF JAMES
I have heard it is quite popular with the younger set, especially the ladies. "Berry's Fairies" are sure to know it backwards and forwards...

EDITH
Walter's fairies? Bah...silly, giggling little bob-haired things
hanging off of Walter and flopping out of their frocks! Eager
to discuss literature, are they? We shall see –

EDITH snatches up Gatsby *again.*

The Great Gatsby. Hm...the Henry James I knew would have
used a book like this for kindling and whistled while he
prodded the ashes.

GHOST OF JAMES
Death has a way of tempering one's cynicism. Besides, it
may resonate.

EDITH
And then I - what? Ask him to call? Would we even like one
another?

GHOST OF JAMES
Whether or not you end up liking him is beside the point.
I've always been interested in people but I've never liked
them.

EDITH
Well what would we do?

GHOST OF JAMES
I leave it to your discretion...still, there are few hours in life
more agreeable than the one dedicated to afternoon tea.

EDITH
Tea.

GHOST OF JAMES
Perhaps you might help him. And...who knows? He may
even help you.

EDITH faces away.

EDITH
How might he do that?

GHOST OF JAMES
In the same way that you have helped me.

*Beat. EDITH turns. GHOST OF JAMES is gone. EDITH sits.
She thinks. She opens the cover to* The Great Gatsby. *She
begins to read.*

SCENE THREE

*The Fitzgeralds' Paris flat. Earlier than the first scene.
Paintings around the room but not as many - they haven't
been painted yet. In the bed, a tangle of limbs beneath the
sheet. On the nightstand, several glasses. A bottle. An alarm
clock rings. FITZGERALD reaches out and turns it off. He
sits up.*

ZELDA
What time is it?

FITZGERALD
Saturday?

Beat.

ZELDA
Time to get up!

ZELDA jumps out of bed in her slip and pulls clothes off the floor.

Quick, Scott, what did you do with the toothbrush?

She finds it in the sheets.

Nevermind.

FITZGERALD
Where are you going?

ZELDA
Brushing
Meeting Lubov Egorova for lunch. You remember her, the famous ballet instructor we met the other night?

FITZGERALD
What for?

ZELDA
We were talking. I told her I'm a dancer.

FITZGERALD
You used to dance.

ZELDA
You haven't written a new story this week. Does that mean you used to write?

Beat.

Damn...forgot to pick up coffee. Do we have anything I can put in my stomach?

FITZGERALD
I think there's half a chocolate bar under the bed...

He reaches below.

Yep. Want some?

ZELDA
Nah, that stuff'll kill you.

FITZGERALD
C'mon, just have a bite...

ZELDA
I said no, Scott. Besides, I'm just now getting my shape back since Scottie was born.

FITZGERALD munches petulantly, notices one of the paintings of several ballerinas with strange, mannish bodies.

FITZGERALD
Hmph. Well, if those pass for ballerina limbs you shouldn't have much to worry about.

ZELDA
You like?

FITZGERALD
I'm confused. Are they men or women?

ZELDA
Yes.

FITZGERALD
Well I think you should cover them up. They'll frighten Scottie if she sees them. And - give her ideas...

ZELDA
Oh, well we mustn't give her ideas...I want her to grow up to be a beautiful little fool. That's the best thing a girl can be, right?

FITZGERALD
If you say so. You know, I really don't think you should be taking up a hobby right now - Scottie barely sees you as it is. She spends so much time with that British nanny she's starting to sound like some damn little cockney.

ZELDA
Pausing
Poor Scottie, she must miss her momma so much.

FITZGERALD
You can walk down the hall and see her.

ZELDA
Oh, I suppose I'll see her at Christmas. Besides, I do spend time with her. Why, didn't I give her a bath just yesterday?

FITZGERALD
You put her in the bidet.

ZELDA
I thought it was the tub! And I made it up to her, I gave her some of my lemonade.

FITZGERALD
That was a gin fizz. Scottie threw up all over the table cloth.

ZELDA
She never even thanked me.

ZELDA rises, dressed.

ZELDA
Well, toodle-oo...

ZELDA walks toward the door. FITZGERALD launches out of the bed and throws himself at her feet.

FITZGERALD
You can't be a ballerina, you'll ruin those perfect feet! And then where am I supposed to worship.

He kisses her feet.

ZELDA
Brushing by
Can't you men ever want to worship us when we actually feel like goddesses?

FITZGERALD
Mocking
Noooooooooooooo - what's this?

FITZGERALD picks an envelope up off the floor between him and ZELDA as she is putting her shoes' heels on at the door.

ZELDA
What?

FITZGERALD
An envelope.

ZELDA
I don't know. Scottie's nanny got the mail. She must have put it there.

FITZGERALD
The Pavillon Colombe!

He reads.

Edith Wharton requests "the pleasure of my company for tea."

ZELDA
She what?

FITZGERALD
She wants to have me for tea!

ZELDA
More likely have you for breakfast. Well you shouldn't.

FITZGERALD
Why the hell not?

ZELDA
After her letter on Gatsby? You'd let that bluestocking patronize you further? I can just picture it now..."Mr. Fitzgerald, your method in taking tea, while crude, shows a primitive kind of potential. I believe one day with hard work and perseverance, you may become a talented tea-taker indeed."

FITZGERALD
Of course, you're right...I should decline.

ZELDA
Good. Take her down a peg.

FITZGERALD
Except...

ZELDA
What?

FITZGERALD
Maybe I should go just to...be able to...laugh about it later.

ZELDA
Are you joking?

FITZGERALD
No. I mean, who knows? Maybe someone who might help
me will be there. And whatever I think of her...she has
cache. Taking tea with her means one has...arrived in a
sense. Maybe you should skip this lunch and come with m -

ZELDA
I - will - not - be - condescended - to!

FITZGERALD
All right! Gee!

ZELDA
And I don't want you hanging around that old woman
either, or any old woman. It'll make you old too and you
won't want to take me dancing anymore. Growing old is
terrible, Scott, we can't do it. Not ever. You and I must die
by the time we're thirty or it'll spoil everything.

FITZGERALD
I'm almost thirty now.

ZELDA moves to go, almost solemnly.

ZELDA
I'll get the rat poison...

FITZGERALD
Zelda.

He pulls her back to him, looks into her eyes.

FITZGERALD
I'll always take you dancing.

Beat. They begin to dance. It turns into something more.

What about your lunch?

ZELDA
We'll be quick.

FITZGERALD
If I didn't know better, I would swear you were using your feminine wiles to keep me here.

ZELDA
Isn't that what we do? I keep you from working and you keep me from living?

FITZGERALD
Is that really how you see us? I think that's incredibly sad.

ZELDA
Don't think...

They kiss. It becomes more passionate.

Scott.

Pause.

Scott...

FITZGERALD
What?

ZELDA
Tell me...

FITZGERALD
I love you...

ZELDA
No...tell me you won't go to that tea...

FITZGERALD
Still passionate
I'm not going to tell you that.

ZELDA
You must. Say it.

FITZGERALD pulls back to study her.

FITZGERALD
No.

ZELDA
Suddenly very angry
I don't see what the big to-do is anyway! It's just going to be
like one of her stuffy literary talks at Queen's Acre with
Henry James and the usual troupe of cake eaters...

Beat.

Oh...Ooooh, I see...

FITZGERALD
What?

ZELDA
Don't worry, I understand completely...

FITZGERALD
You understand what?

ZELDA
The crowd at this tea...it's sure to be awfully festive. All
those artists and poets...and all the knitting and the little
cakes...boy! And here I couldn't figure out why you were so
eager for us to lunch with Gertrude Stein -

FITZGERALD
Now hold on just a minute -

ZELDA
I'm just glad you're ready to come to terms with this side of
you...in fact, maybe I will come along. We can make a day of
it...I'll come in a top hat and tails with a friend and say,
"hello, I'm Zelda and this is my pregnant, Jewish, lesbian
negro chum," and then we'll all dance cheek to cheek until
they send the wagon!

FITZGERALD pulls her close again.

FITZGERALD
Hey, let's speculate about us some more! I hear Scott has
the biggest member of any expat on the continent -

ZELDA
I hear Scott and Ernest Hemingway are having an affair.

Beat.

FITZGERALD
What?

ZELDA
That's what people say, anyway. I must admit I've wondered for a while...normal men don't get voted prettiest in the class-

FITZGERALD
Goddamn it Zelda! Are we back to this again? Because I really won't have it. You may be dealing with your own loathsome daydreams - inclinations, even...but you will not drag me down with you, understand?

Beat.

FITZGERALD
I said do you understand?

ZELDA begins to laugh, giggles at first, then full out guffaws. FITZGERALD turns away in disgust.

Damn. I just don't know what you want of me, Zelda.

Pause.

Zelda!

Just as suddenly, ZELDA stops laughing. She is having another "moment." She stares. FITZGERALD turns.

FITZGERALD
Zelda? Is it happening again?

He moves to her. Beat.

ZELDA
Do you know what she calls us?

FITZGERALD
Who?

ZELDA
Gertrude Stein. She calls us the "Lost Generation."

FITZGERALD
Calls who?

ZELDA
You, me, Hemingway, all of us...

FITZGERALD
She came up with that because we got side-tracked off the highway on our road trip down the Riviera. It doesn't mean anything. You know that right?

Pause.

Right?

Beat.

ZELDA
I have to take a bath.

In a flash, ZELDA is at the bathroom door, her hand on the knob.

FITZGERALD
Zelda, stop. You can't! You have your lunch to get to, remember?

ZELDA turns the knob, opens the door. FITZGERALD runs to the front door and turns the knob.

FITZERALD

If you step in that bathroom I'm leaving. I'll walk straight to Edith Wharton's and see if she wants that tea right now, I mean it.

Standoff. ZELDA slips into the bathroom and shuts the door. Short pause, then FITZGERALD hurries back into the room.

Zelda! Zelda, what are you doing? Come out, you can't do this again! I won't go through it again. Zelda!

He pounds on the door. Beat. He moves around the room, looking for something to break the door down with. The door swings opens just as he returns with an end table. ZELDA stands there, a provocative grin on her face. FITZGERALD lowers the end table a bit, heaving. ZELDA pulls him to her. He drops the table in surprise as the door slams shut. END OF SCENE.

SCENE FOUR

Pavillon Colombe. GROSSIE is dusting swiftly, with EDITH cleaning beside her.

EDITH
Quickly, Grossie!

GROSSIE
I can't go any faster, Edie. I'll send the duster straight through the selves...There, now I've done it - tore the feathers clean off. Back in a moment.

EDITH
Well, hurry! We must move diligently -

GROSSIE exits just as GHOST OF JAMES appears.

GHOST OF JAMES
Diligently! Well, I suppose I never could resist an adverb.
They are the only qualifications I much respect.

EDITH
Not now Henry! I must concentrate.

GHOST OF JAMES
Of course. That table requires immediate ministrations.

EDITH
Yes.

GHOST OF JAMES
Your zeal pertains to tidiness alone.

EDITH
Quite.

GHOST OF JAMES
And has absolutely nothing to do with Walter coming to
call.

Beat.

EDITH
If you must know, Walter happened to phone that he is in
Paris for the day and wishes to call.

GHOST OF JAMES
Well this is quite the welcome.

EDITH
It is no more than the hospitality I would show any guest.

EDITH attacks the table with polish.

GHOST OF JAMES
Well do not let me interrupt. I only want to be of service.
Perhaps I can help think of ways to entertain him. For
instance, what shall you talk about?

EDITH
Literature I imagine. He shall be starved for intelligent
conversation after all his fairies, and I am eager to discuss
French novels...I have never seen writers who can manage
romance without stooping to sentimentality like the
French..."l'amour, c'est l'espace et le temps rendus sensibles
au coeur..."

GHOST OF JAMES
Ah...Marcel Proust.

EDITH
Marvelous man!

Beat.

GHOST OF JAMES
You know, Proust was not so different from these new
writers you so lament...his Remembrance of Things Past
routinely depicts men "together" with women, and women
with women...and men with m - mmm...men.

EDITH
Well maybe it just seems more tasteful when the French do
it.

GHOST OF JAMES
Hmmm...well, perhaps literature is not the best course.
Walter is an outdoor type, he may want to discuss

GHOST OF JAMES
Continued
something more, ah...constitutional.

EDITH
What?

GHOST OF JAMES
Oh, you know...nautical.

EDITH
Henry, what are you prattling on about?

GHOST OF JAMES
I want you to invite Walter on your Aegean Cruise.

Beat.

EDITH
Get out.

GHOST OF JAMES
Puss...

EDITH
I haven't the time for this now, Henry, you will have to
haunt me later.

GHOST OF JAMES
I cannot leave, I am...helping you clean!

*Pause. GHOST OF JAMES slowly picks up a cloth and
noncommittally dabs at a shade with it.*

EDITH
Then stay, but please no more foolishness. Walter and I

EDITH
Continued
have been through this all before. Even when we were
children our mothers didn't approve.

EDITH goes back to the table.

Mother loved Teddy, however. She must have, she was so
overcome by our approaching nuptials she left my name
clear off the invitations.

GHOST OF JAMES
Oh bother Teddy and bother your mother! We are
discussing Walter. And now with nothing standing in the
way, is it not time you both stopped hanging fire and -

EDITH
Calling off
Grossie! Ah - where is she? Nevermind, I shall finish
myself.

GHOST OF JAMES
You know this is not necessary, Edith. Your houses are
always breathtaking. You have impeccable taste.

Beat.

Though here is one thing I cannot understand...these heavy
curtains. The exact indulgent kind of excess you once railed
against.

EDITH
I have amended my view on those. I hated the thought of
my mother's set...hidden by their curtains while they peer
out at the rest of the world, judging. But now I see the value

EDITH
Continued
of privacy. And the light...it fades all the furniture if it gets
in -

GHOST OF JAMES
Sighing
Must we all become our mothers...

Pause.

GHOST OF JAMES
Shall I open them or not?

EDITH
Which would Walter prefer?

GHOST OF JAMES
Whichever makes you the most comfortable, I am sure.

Pause.

EDITH
Leave them closed.

He does.

GHOST OF JAMES
Edith, at least promise you will consider it -

EDITH
Walter and I are friends, Henry. I expect nothing more nor
less from him.

GHOST OF JAMES
Of course.

EDITH
Walter and I understand one another. That is all.

GHOST OF JAMES
Without question.

EDITH
We share a deep, profound, abiding sense of –

GHOST OF JAMES
Love?

EDITH
Sympathy! Which shall continue to bind us no matter how far from each other we may roam. But remarriage? That is absolutely, positively the furthest thing from my mind.

GHOST OF JAMES
I never mentioned remarriage.

Beat. There is a knock at the door. EDITH'S face is radiant with joy. She arranges herself grandly. Suddenly:

EDITH
Henry...

Pause.

I will...consider it.

GHOST OF JAMES sits, pleased. GROSSIE enters.

GROSSIE
Miss. You have a guest.

EDITH
Please show him in -

GROSSIE
Mr. Edward Wharton.

WHARTON enters, frighteningly disheveled. GROSSIE exits.

EDITH
Edward?

WHARTON
Hello, Edith, dear.

EDITH
Edward, what are you doing here?

WHARTON
I have returned from my trip to Switzerland.

EDITH
They let you go on your own? Where is your doctor?

WHARTON
Doctor? Why do I need a doctor, dear? Never felt better in my life.

EDITH
But how did you get here?

WHARTON
I walked. You see? I am in top shape! Except for this toothache...

EDITH
Oh no...Oh Edward, no no no...

WHARTON
And now that I am better, I thought that maybe I could stay for a while, take over our affairs again. I know I had a bad run of it with the finances the last time, but this time -

EDITH
Edward, you are not well –

WHARTON
Maybe you and I could be together for a while -

EDITH
Edward, you should not be here. You are ill, you must go back!

WHARTON
Go back? But why would I go back? Unless...

Beat.

I am wrong, is that it? My head is wrong, I mean.

EDITH
Edward...

WHARTON
No, that is it...I am losing my mind.

EDITH
Perhaps you should sit down for a moment -

WHARTON
Oh God...I just...they tell me I am getting better, the
specialists...

GHOST OF JAMES
Oh, the play I could write on "specialists..."

WHARTON looks up.

WHARTON
What was that?

EDITH
What Edward?

WHARTON
I thought I heard a voice...

Pause.

They are wrong, the specialists...about my getting better...I
am not at home at all, am I?

Beat.

EDITH
Of course you are. Welcome home, Edward.

WHARTON
Home?

EDITH
Yes. Please come and take off your heavy coat. Catherine?

GROSSIE enters quickly.

GROSSIE
Yes?

EDITH
Would you please take Mr. Wharton's coat and then call up
the...hotel in Switzerland and tell them where Mr. Wharton
is. Then see about sending a car around to retrieve him.

GROSSIE
Right away...

GROSSIE takes WHARTON'S coat and exits.

WHARTON
Yes, yes...I am home.

EDITH
Of course you are. Come, let me draw you a bath and then
straight to bed. I will have supper brought to you.

WHARTON
Oh, I do not think that will be necessary. I feel a new man. I
really do Edith. I knew I would feel better after I saw you.
And it makes such a difference to be useful. I will be a help
with the finances now, won't I?

EDITH
Of course you will be, Edward. Thank you.

WHARTON
There now! Happy to be of service. You see, sometimes a
wife still needs her husband.

EDITH
I am grateful.

WHARTON
I am a good husband.

EDITH
Edward.

WHARTON
I am a good husband.

EDITH
Teddy.

WHARTON
Hm?

Pause.

EDITH
A car will be here for you this evening, Teddy.

WHARTON
Are they coming to fix my toothache?

EDITH
Your teeth are false now, Teddy. You do not have a toothache.

WHARTON
Ah. Well I suppose I shall have to say goodbye again for a time. You must not be too upset, though. Your Teddy will return to you soon. I know how hard it is for a wife when her husband is away.

EDITH
It is - very hard.

EDITH leads him out.

EDITH
Come. I will join you in a moment.

WHARTON exits. EDITH turns to the telephone. Beat.

Operateur? Oui. Deux...deux...neuf...quatre. Merci.

Pause.

Walter? Yes, Edith...have I caught you in time?

Pause.

EDITH
No, something has come up. I am afraid I cannot see you
today. But I am free tomorrow! Would it be possible to-

Pause.

Leaving in the morning. Of course. But you shall come
through again soon, I am sure.

Pause.

I see.

Pause.

I understand...it is my fault entirely - the busy authoress...

Pause.

Goodbye Walter.

EDITH hangs up the phone. Beat. EDITH turns to GHOST OF JAMES, but he is gone. She is alone. END OF SCENE.

SCENE FIVE

The publishing offices of Charles Scribner in New York. SCRIBNER sits at his desk, reviewing manuscripts. There is a knock at the door.

SCRIBNER
Come in.

Secretary enters.

SECRETARY
Mr. Scribner, your 4 o'clock is here.

SCRIBNER
It's 3:15.

SECRETARY
She's early. Shall I tell her to -

EDITH sweeps into the room, removing her furs.

SCRIBNER
Thank you, that will do!

As SECRETARY exits, EDITH piles the furs on top of her and moves to the desk. SECRETARY scurries out.

Edith!

EDITH drops a manuscript heavily on the desk.

Beat.

SCRIBNER
Lovely to see you as always. And ahead of schedule...

EDITH
I doubted just an hour would be sufficient to address all the errors I discovered in the latest proofs.

SCRIBNER
Edith, I can assure you such errors are purely in your mind. Why I reviewed the proofs myse –

EDITH
Charles, I hope I will not have to remind you that Appleton has shown interest in my new book as well.

SCRIBNER
I am surprised to hear you mention it, Edith. Of course, I assumed Appleton would be interested after you gave them *The Age of Innocence*, and it won the Pulitzer.

EDITH
You seem to imply I did you a wrong in that.

SCRIBNER
Well I am sorry to hear you have been so dissatisfied with us -

EDITH
Oh come, Charles! I like you more than anyone in publishing. You have integrity and clarity. But that does not mean you sell my books. And I am a business woman. If I weren't I would write about what is pressing on my mind and on my heart instead of more claptrap to match the new optimism America is peddling. Progress! Moving forward!

SCRIBNER
Well what do you want to write about, Edith?

EDITH
What?

Pause.

The War! I want to write about the War!

SCRIBNER
The war is over.

EDITH
Is it? Ever since the armistice I wonder, will it ever be over? Will we ever be "us" again? But you cannot write about such a question...it isn't "nice." So I gave them *The Age of Innocence* and it won the Pulitzer, and it made a lot of money. I am willing to sell out, Charles, but the price needs to be right. That is where you come in.

SCRIBNER
So you want us to market your books as Appleton does? Like tabloid fodder in between advertisements for vacuums and talcum powder?

EDITH
It gets readers' attention.

SCRIBNER
It is tacky, Edith. And you know it to be as well. I do not believe that is how you want me to market your work; you are far too well bred for that.

EDITH
Breeding must give way to necessity sometimes, Charles, or

EDITH
Continued
one falls by the wayside. Why that is the entire theme of my
novels! Novels, I might add, that you insist on spoiling with
those garish illustrations...

SCRIBNER
Ah, but Edith..."illustrations sell."

Beat.

The fact is that despite your desire to sell, a part of you - the
best part I have always thought...would rather lose than win
like that.

EDITH
Perhaps. And it is your job as my publisher to compensate
for that tendency.

SCRIBNER
Believe me. I know what people are saying. I know they
think me "old fashioned..."

EDITH
I should say so!

SCRIBNER
But I have been there for you, Edith. Do not give up on us. I
will always fight for you.

Beat.

I could bring up that plot of ours on Henry James's behalf,
though I would be loath to mention it -

EDITH
I would be loath to hear it mentioned -

SCRIBNER
When he was not selling any books and was crippled by
depression...and you asked me to take out of your royalties
a massive advance to offer him for an important American
novel, he said it "seemed strange." But I never gave you
away.

EDITH
But he found out anyway, and it almost destroyed our
friendship. Moral of the story...the best of intentions are
irrelevant. Honor and patriotism are good for novels, but
mustard gas wins the war. If one wants to keep up with
these new writers, one must always have victory in mind.

SCRIBNER
But you are keeping up! How you are! Why young
Fitzgerald practically adores you.

EDITH
Ah yes, I remember Mr. Fitzgerald well. Wrote a rather
scathing caricature of me, if I recall.

SCRIBNER
Oh, Edith. You are each viewing the other through the
wrong end of a telescope.

EDITH
How do you mean?

SCRIBNER
He just wants to get your attention! He is like a child on a
diving board.

EDITH
Utter nonsense.

Beat.

You know I always did think imitation the sincerest form of flattery. Do you really think he might look up to me?

Suddenly, FITZGERALD bursts into the office and flings himself at EDITH'S feet.

FITZGERALD
You are a goddess!

SCRIBNER
Mr. Fitzgerald! I, er - that is - we are in a meeting! And you are to be meeting with Max Perkins down the hall, yes?

FITZGERALD
Perhaps, but fate brought me to this office instead, to bask in the presence of true genius!

FITZGERALD kisses the hem of EDITH'S dress.

EDITH
Mr. Fitzgerald - that is quite enough.

EDITH retrieves her coat.

Charles, thank you for your time, I think your current marketing strategy will be sufficient.

SCRIBNER
Are - are you certai -

EDITH sweeps past.

EDITH
I shall see myself out.

Beat. SCRIBNER is speechless.

FITZGERALD
Would now be a good time to discuss my next advance?

END OF SCENE.

SCENE SIX

Scribner's office from the other side of the door. EDITH enters the waiting room and moves to SECRETARY.

SECRETARY
Good afternoon. Did you have an appointment with Mr. Scrib -

EDITH
Tell Charles Edith Wharton is here to see him.

SECRETARY
Mrs. Wharton, it's such an honor! I've read your books since-

EDITH
Just tell him I am waiting.

SECRETARY
O - of course.

Secretary rises.

Just a moment.

SECRETARY enters the office.

SECRETARY (O.S.)
Mr. Scribner, your 4 o'clock is here.

SCRIBNER (O.S.)
It's 3:15.

SECRETARY (O.S.)
She's early. Shall I tell her to –

EDITH enters the office.

SCRIBNER (O.S.)
Thank you, that will do...

Pause.

SCRIBNER (O.S.)
Edith!

SECRETARY enters loaded with furs as the door shuts behind her. She hangs them on a rack and sits at her desk. Beat.

SECRETARY
Bitch.

FITZGERALD and PERKINS enter, talking.

Hello, Mr. Perkins!

PERKINS
Hello, Fanny. Lovely day we're having.

SECRETARY
I'll say it is!

*SECRETARY goes back to work. FITZGERALD and
PERKINS move aside.*

FITZGERALD
Lovely eyes, that Fanny.

PERKINS
You should see her fanny.

Beat.

So, Scott, you didn't make the trip all the way to New York
just to take a dip in the steno pool. What can I do for you?

FITZGERALD
Well, to be honest, Max, money has been a little tight. I
wanted to run some new material by you - see if you might
be interested in the usual advance arrangement.

PERKINS
Got another jazz tale in the works, eh? I suppose we could
work something out -

*Beat. FITZGERALD pulls out Zelda's diary and hands it to
PERKINS. PERKINS opens it and reads.*

Is this Zelda's diar -

FITZGERALD
Yes, it is.

PERKINS
Hm.

Pause.

PERKINS
Not bad. Florid style. Lush almost.

FITZGERALD
It has some merit, that's what I told her. My question is, do you think there might be a market for something like this, say under the title "Diary of a Popular Girl" or something?

PERKINS
Why, sure! It's like a glimpse into the life of a flapper. It would fly off the shelves. Doesn't even look like it needs many changes.

FITZGERALD
That's what I thought, that's what I thought...

PERKINS
Of course, I don't know if just Zelda's name on the byline would be enough to get it in print. I might have to add you as well, just to make it move. But then I'm sure you would be contributing -

FITZGERALD
Oh, you misunderstand me. Zelda doesn't want her name on this at all. It would embarrass her, see. If it flopped, she couldn't take it. Awfully sensitive about her writing.

PERKINS
Oh?

FITZGERALD
Yes.

Pause.

FITZGERALD
Continued
I'll split the advance with her if it gets accepted of course.

PERKINS
Of course.

Pause.

Let me see what I can do.

FITZGERALD
Wonderful. Wonderful. Oh, and one more thing Max...

PERKINS
Yes?

FITZGERALD
Well, I know it's a bother, but the sweet girl has gotten it into her head to try a novel of her own. I don't want to put you through too much trouble, but if you wouldn't mind looking it over, sending her a little note...

PERKINS
Of course! I'd be happy to! I'll even be glad to publish it if I think it's ready.

FITZGERALD
Oh, let's not get ahead of ourselves. She probably wouldn't want that anyway, she's far too shy, insecure about her talent and all that. But maybe just a note that she shows real promise. I just ask that you don't critique her too hard or come down like you would on a professional.

PERKINS
Oh, I doubt that will be necessary.

PERKINS holds up the diary.

PERKINS
If what I read here is any indication -

FITZGERALD
Just let her down easy, Max, that's all I'm asking. Oh, and Max, let me know if any of her novel touches on the same material I was planning on using for *Tender is the Night.* Being married, we go to so many of the same parties...bound to be some overlap. I just don't want to make her look silly if we write about the same incident and my version makes hers look...well, I'm sure I've made myself clear.

Beat.

Am I being clear?

PERKINS
Practically transparent.

FITZGERALD
I'm glad.

PERKINS
Well listen, Scott, it's been wonderful catching up but I really must be getting back to it.

FITZGERALD
Of course, of course! Thanks for squeezing me in.

PERKINS holds up the diary.

PERKINS
I'll, uh...get this back to you.

FITZGERALD
Take your time! I'm in no hurry.

PERKINS
Oh, and Scott, if you see Hemingway anytime soon, tell him congratulations in advance for me. That new book he's finishing, *The Sun also Rises*, is poised to take the literary world by storm in a few months.

FITZGERALD
That soon?

PERKINS
Boy, he doesn't churn 'em out like you, Scott, but when he strikes it's like a bolt of lightning. Better watch out or he'll eat you alive, you poor son-of-a-bitch!

PERKINS exits. Long beat. FITZGERALD turns and sees SECRETARY, stretching her back. He approaches.

FITZGERALD
Well hi there...Fanny? Was it?

SECRETARY
Uh huh.

FITZGERALD
Well listen Fanny, I'm stuck here for the rest of the afternoon with nothing much to do, and was wondering if you had any interest in grabbing a coffee with me.

SECRETARY
Oh, I'd love to Mr. Fitzgerald. It's almost my break, just let me pop in and see if Mr. Scribner is done in there with Mrs. Wharton and I'll be -

FITZGERALD
Done with who?

SECRETARY
Mrs. Wharton -

FITZGERALD
Edith Wharton? Is in that office...right now?

SECRETARY
Uh huh...so if you don't mind waiting for just a se - Mr.
Fitzgerald!

FITZGERALD throws the door open and bursts into the office.

FITZGERALD (O.S)
You are a goddess!

The door closes, we hear the muffled conversation from before as SECRETARY leans in to hear. Suddenly EDITH emerges from the office grandly. SECRETARY hurries to her desk and sits, eyes forward as EDITH retrieves her furs from the hook. EDITH turns and eyes her. Beat.

EDITH
You there. Yes you - you are what they call a...oh, what is
the phrase...a "bright young thing?"

SECRETARY
I - I suppose so, Mrs. Wharton...

EDITH
And what do you think of this Mr. Fitzgerald?

SECRETARY
Scott Fitzgerald? Oh, he's very popular. And talented, too -
why all the girls I know are just mad for him -

EDITH
And does he enjoy tea?

SECRETARY
Ah - tea? Well, I guess he would. Especially if he were to be
invited by someone like you, that he really respected -

EDITH
Yes, I see what you mean -

SECRETARY
Barreling on
You know, I've always dreamed of sitting down to tea with a
great author like you, Mrs. Wharton, and just talking about
novels and poetry and, oh gosh, all sorts of things that -

EDITH
That will do.

SECRETARY
O - kay.

*EDITH begins to exit. Slows. She turns to SECRETARY.
Slowly, she returns to SECRETARY'S desk, picks up a pen,
and scrawls her autograph across the notepad. EDITH tears
the sheet off and hands it to SECRETARY.*

Th - thank you Mrs. Wharton...

*EDITH nods and exits. SECRETARY looks at the autograph.
She turns and looks at the door to the office, then out.*

END OF ACT ONE.

ACT TWO

SCENE ONE

The Fitzgeralds' Paris flat. The place is a shambles. Bottles line the floor and wall. FITZGERALD enters with CAMPBELL.

CAMPBELL
Glad you were in, Fitz, haven't seen you in ages! Boy when I ran into you and Zelda on the Champs Elysees you could have knocked me over with a feather -

FITZGERALD
I'm always in for another Princeton man, Camp. I'm gonna make myself a drink, that jake with you?

CAMPBELL
It's, uh...2:00 in the afternoon, Fitz.

Beat.

Oh what the heck, that's why you're the famous writer I guess. If you say it's up to date to drink at 2:00, I guess it must be!

FITZGERALD pours gin into a shaker and stirs.

FITZGERALD
I always need a pick-me-up this time of day, Camp. Insomnia. A drink's the only thing that can wake me up or put me to sleep anymore.

CAMPBELL
Well how do you know which one it's gonna do?

FITZGERALD
The dosage.

CAMPBELL chuckles.

CAMPBELL
Hey, that's kinda clever.

FITZGERALD
I got a million more written down over there in my "Ledger:
Outline of my Life." Got some neat ideas for my novel
written down in there too if you wanna hear.

CAMPBELL
Huh...you got any pictures of Zelda in there? Then you
could call it "Ledger: Outline of my Wife."

*The men laugh. ZELDA appears in the doorway of the
bathroom, draping herself against the frame in profile. She
is in one of her organdy Southern belle dresses, somewhat
burned.*

ZELDA
Drawling
I thought I heard a man's voice in here. Lawton Campbell,
as I live and breathe...

CAMPBELL
How do you do, Zelda...

ZELDA
Awfully mean of Scott to try and keep you all to
himself...why he only met you at Princeton, but you and I
are from Montgomery - and blood is thicker than gin!

CAMPBELL
Wow, that's some get-up!

ZELDA
Isn't it kee-yoot? I'm masquerading as myself.

CAMPBELL
Now what do you mean by that, I wond - why Zelda, your dress is burnt!

FITZGERALD
Here's that drink, Camp!

CAMPBELL
Say, don't you wanna shake those, Fitz?

FITZGERALD pushes the glass on CAMPBELL.

FITZGERALD
Oh, no. I always stir. In this household, we do not bruise our gin.

ZELDA
No, just our wives.

ZELDA turns forward. She has a rather nasty looking black eye. CAMPBELL sets his drink aside.

CAMPBELL
Zelda! What happened to your eye?

ZELDA
Oh, clumsy me. Walked into a door. Or fell down the stairs. Or Scott hit me in the face.

Pause.

ZELDA
It was the stairs.

Beat. CAMPBELL laughs loudly. FITZGERALD downs his drink. Pours another. ZELDA dabs makeup on.

CAMPBELL
Hit you in the face! Sure, sure! Well, eye or no eye, you're just glowin' - both of you. When I saw you on the street I thought, "who's that handsome couple that looks like they just stepped out of the sun?"

ZELDA
I designed that get-up myself - it's my Joan of Arc dress.

CAMPBELL
Well let's hope you don't end up like her.

ZELDA
Oh, it wouldn't be so bad.

CAMPBELL
Zelda, Joan of Arc was burnt at the stake!

ZELDA
Yes, but at least she got to be tied up first. And this is my "Elizabeth Arden" face...

Poses.

ZELDA
They used it for the cover of "Hearst International." I'll send you a copy if you like...

CAMPBELL
And how! That is, if it's jake with you, Scott.

FITZGERALD
Sure. Jake.

CAMPBELL
You know it's not just the clothes, though, there's
something electric about you, Zelda...maybe that new
marcel wave -

ZELDA
Well, I did drop the baby weight from Scottie - Scott was so
relieved. He didn't like his wife losing her figure at all...

CAMPBELL
You lose your figure - go on...

ZELDA
It's true! Scott likes me looking just like I did when he
carried me off to New York - thin, pink, and helpless.

CAMPBELL
Fitz, you sly old fox.

ZELDA
Well, you know women, Camp. Sometimes they just want a
man to throw them over his shoulder and whisk them away.

CAMPBELL
That a fact, Zelda?

ZELDA
Well, I suppose that depends on if you believe the Sabine
Women were raped or not.

CAMPBELL
I see, I see. Now...what's a Sabine Woman?

Beat.

ZELDA
Anyway, I can see why Scott would choose New York - so many captains of industry to rub elbows with. Money does matter to him so.

FITZGERALD
You know, the rich are different than you and me, Camp...

CAMPBELL
How's that?

FITZGERALD
They have more money!

The men laugh. ZELDA joins in.

ZELDA
Oh! I forgot all about that joke. Funniest thing Ernest has ever said. That man is nothing if not quotable.

FITZGERALD glares.

CAMPBELL
Oh, that's Hemingway's. Thought you just came up with it Fitz. "They have more money," that's a good one...

ZELDA
Well if you want to hear a good one - you remember when Scott and I toured Rome?

CAMPBELL
Rome?

FITZGERALD
She got it into her head to see Italy while reading Henry James...says she can't stand those old writers but can't wait to go wherever they tell her...

ZELDA
Oh, listen to Scott...you know he's thinking of adding a scene with a golden bowl in *Tender is the Night*, just like in that James novel, oh, what's it called... *The Golden Bowl?*

FITZGERALD laughs nervously.

FITZGERALD
That's nothing, dear. Just paying my respects...

ZELDA
Really? Well pay any more respect, and you'll be sued for plagiarism.

CAMPBELL
So what did you think, Zelda?

ZELDA
Hm? Of what?

CAMPBELL
Of Rome!

FITZGERALD
Oh, of Rome! Well, I can sum it up for you in a sentence. We wrote a letter to Max Perkins, my publisher over at Scribner's. You know what it said? It said -

ZELDA
It said "Roman ruins are better in France!" I thought of it. Wasn't that clever?

CAMPBELL
What a wit on this one! Go on...

ZELDA
One time someone asked me if *The Beautiful and Damned*
was based on me and Scott. Do you know what I said? Tell
him Scott.

FITZGERALD
She said -

ZELDA
I said, "you bet it is...I'm beautiful and Scott's damned!"

CAMPBELL
Laughing
Oh! "I'm beautiful...he's damned..." This little lady sure can
turn a phrase. Hey Fitz, maybe she should take a crack at
writing...

ZELDA
Well, wouldn't that just be a lark? Maybe someday Edith
Wharton can congratulate me over my latest novel.

FITZGERALD
To Campbell
I just got a letter from Edith Wharton over Gatsby.

CAMPBELL
You don't say! What did she say in the letter?

FITZGERALD
Oh, who can recall? She's passe. Only beat Sinclair Lewis for
the Pulitzer in '23 because the committee pulled some
strings for her. Lewis calls it the "Main Street robbery." Not
sure she wasn't behind it herself.

CAMPBELL
You think *Main Street* deserved it over *The Age of Innocence?*

FITZGERALD
Maybe. Not a bad novel *Main Street.*

CAMPBELL
I just read his latest, *Babbitt,* too. Dedicated it to Wharton herself, come to think of it. Damn fine book.

FITZGERALD
Damn fine.

ZELDA
I thought you called *Babbitt* "rotten."

FITZGERALD
I never said th -

ZELDA
No, I must be mistaken. How could a novel that sells 300,000 copies be rotten after all? By the way Scott, how many copies did Gatsby sell? 50,000, was it? No wait...49...

Beat. CAMPBELL laughs once, sharply.

FITZGERALD
How's that rash, Zelda?

CAMPBELL
Rash?

FITZGERALD
Zelda's got a nasty case of eczema. Covers her whole chest. Bit of an affliction, really.

ZELDA
More of a nuisance. And losing its hold over me. Every day I
work it out of my system a little more.

*ZELDA holds FITZGERALD'S gaze. Smacks her gum.
Maybe blows a bubble.*

FITZGERALD
Chewing gum again, darling?

ZELDA
To CAMPBELL
He hates when I chew gum too, says it makes me look just
like a cow.

CAMPBELL
Oh, I'm sure that's...not true -

FITZGERALD puts his palm out.

FITZGERALD
Here, why don't you give it to me -

*ZELDA swallows the gum. FITZGERALD moves away,
refills his drink.*

ZELDA
No drawl
In answer to your questions, Lawton, writing simply isn't a
viable pursuit at the moment. Why I'm a wife and mother,
and I have a home to take care of. I get my kicks cooking
and cleaning just like everybody else.

Beat, everyone does a take at the room.

CAMPBELL
Well, Zelda, that's good to hear. So many women are
dissatisfied, nowadays. Still, it doesn't mean you shouldn't
branch out and try new things now and then.

ZELDA
Well, I did have a few ideas for a novel, but they didn't pan
out. Scott's the writer in the family. You know he was
named after his cousin Francis Scott Key, who wrote the
Star Spangled Banner? I mean when your name is a hand me
down from someone that famous, you're bound to
accomplish something or other...

CAMPBELL
Did you start writing young, Fitz?

FITZGERALD
No, not seriously until college, actually.

ZELDA
It was after Princeton dropped him from the football team.

CAMPBELL
Fitz went out for football?

ZELDA
Sure he did! Cut the first day though - too small.

FITZGERALD
Well, you know what they say about Princetonians who
aren't any good at football - they become famous writers.

ZELDA
Mm - who says that?

FITZGERALD
Overlapping
All right, dear -

ZELDA
Accelerating
Oh wait, I do remember something, only when I heard it, it was "what happens to Princetonians who are good at football?"

CAMPBELL
What's that?

ZELDA
They become Yalies!

FITZGERALD
Zelda -

ZELDA
Quickly, to CAMPBELL
Anyway, I'm taking up art again. I'm doing a picture in the bathroom right now. Scottie's out with the nanny and I borrowed her crayons!

FITZGERALD
You borrowed Scottie's...

FITZGERALD moves toward the bathroom but ZELDA quickly shuts the door. Beat.

Hey, wanna see some of my pictures from the war, Camp?

FITZGERALD jumps up and retrieves an album and sits on the side of CAMPBELL'S chair.

CAMPBELL
Uh, s - sure Fitz.

FITZGERALD
Here's me at Camp Sheridan in uniform...here's the entire division...

He flips the page.

And what do you think of this one here?

CAMPBELL
Why, that's a man with his head blown away...

FITZGERALD
Yeah...

CAMPBELL
Is everything...all right, Fitz?

FITZGERALD
Oh, sure - everything's fine. Zelda's just a little under the weather. We both are. Bills stacking up, you know, and the novel's taking longer than I'd hoped. But I'm confident in a month or so I'll have a first draft knocked out that -

A picture slides under the bathroom door. Beat. CAMPBELL picks it up.

CAMPBELL
Zelda, did you do this?

ZELDA (O.S.)
Maaaaaay-beeeeee!

CAMPBELL looks at the picture.

FITZGERALD
I'm so sorry, Camp, she's just...

CAMPBELL
It's good!

FITZGERALD
What? What is it?

CAMPBELL
A picture. A naked figure in a giant champagne glass. Flat
chest, bobbed hair. Almost can't tell the sex or age at all.
Could be a self-portrait, or you, or Scottie even. Huh...

FITZGERALD
Well, I haven't bobbed my hair for quite some time...

CAMPBELL
You know, it's funny...the way the figure is positioned on its
knees, peering over the rim...do you think she's having a
ball or trying to escape? Quite a gift your wife has.

FITZGERALD
Yes, I've noticed that lately.

CAMPBELL
What?

FITZGERALD
Zelda is going crazy and calling it genius. I'm going broke
and calling it whatever comes to mind -

CAMPBELL checks his watch.

CAMPBELL
Oh! Damn it all, Fitz, I didn't realize it was getting so late. I have an appointment. Gotta run. Stop by again soon?

FITZGERALD
Of course, old sport, anytime you like.

CAMPBELL
Well then.

CAMPBELL hands FITZGERALD the picture and slaps him on the shoulder.

Oh, and Fitz, tell Zelda I said goodbye.

CAMPBELL exits. Beat.

FITZGERALD
Zelda!

The door to the bathroom slowly opens. ZELDA emerges. FITZGERALD turns to face her, angry, but stops when he sees her. She looks completely empty.

Zelda? What is it?

ZELDA
The mania...what I feel when we're at a party, when I lift up my skirt and dance, when we do something crazy...it's gone.

FITZGERALD
But what's wrong?

ZELDA
What's wrong is I'm seeing that this is what's underneath!

Beat.

ZELDA
I used to think this feeling, this...vacancy inside me, that it was just a slip, that I had gone under but at any moment I could break the surface again. But what if this is it? What if this - this is lucidity? What if this is when I'm seeing things clearly and it's the other me who's the fake, who doesn't really exist? I don't know if I can bear it! I thought if I laughed enough, and danced enough, and was gay enough that I'd be safe...that it would skip me somehow...I don't know why I thought I could escape it - I don't why I thought - I - I don't know what I thought...

FITZGERALD
Zelda...it's all right...

ZELDA
Oh Scott! Am I cracking up? I don't want to lose my mind, I don't...

FITZGERALD
Zelda, we'll get through this...I'll stop drinking so much, I promise. And you can paint if it helps!

ZELDA
It helps! Anything helps! Anything where I can express myself!

FITZGERALD
Then paint you shall.

Beat.

FITZGERALD
I'll even have a chat with Max Perkins on my trip to New York next week and see what we can do about getting some work of yours published under your own byline.

ZELDA looks at him.

ZELDA
Thank you. Thank you thank you thank you! Oh Goofo, you're my one true jelly bean, you really are!

FITZGERALD
Always.

ZELDA
And I'm your Sally...

FITZGERALD
Sally?

ZELDA
For I am a salamander, the mythical Salamander that can walk through flames and emerge unscathed...as long as I have you.

She buries herself in him, clutching at him like a doll. As he holds her, he looks down at her drawing in his hand. His smile slips - just a notch. END OF SCENE.

SCENE TWO

Pavillon Colombe. EDITH is leading CHANLER inside from the garden. Tea with Fitzgerald has just ended.

CHANLER
Thank you for the tea, Mrs. Wharton. And such a lovely garden...

EDITH
So glad to hear you say so, Mr. Chanler. And please give your mother my regards. Daisy is one of my oldest and dearest friends.

CHANLER
I will do that. And shall I wait for Scott to...

EDITH
I believe Mr. Fitzgerald found his own way out. Goodbye, Teddy. Please feel free to visit anytime.

CHANLER
Goodbye.

CHANLER exits. EDITH shuts the door just as GROSSIE enters with her apron full of broken shards of vase. She shakes her head at EDITH.

GROSSIE
Shame about this vase, Edie. Been in the family for generations. It was your mother's favorite, you know...

EDITH
It certainly is, Grossie. It certainly is. A loss.

Beat.

GROSSIE
Ah, well. Ugly old thing. Dinner will be served in an hour.

EDITH
I shall be writing until then.

GROSSIE exits.

Oh, and Grossie?

Beat. GROSSIE is gone. EDITH goes to her desk and opens her ledger, where she writes something down. She then sits and begins to type at the typewriter. GHOST OF JAMES appears.

EDITH
"It was on a bright day of midwinter, in New York. The little girl who eventually became me, but as yet was neither me nor anybody else in particular...was going for a walk with her father -"

GHOST OF JAMES glances down at the ledger and reads what is written there.

GHOST OF JAMES
"To tea, Teddy Chanler and Scott Fitzgerald, the novelist...horrible."

EDITH
You startled me -

GHOST OF JAMES
Why Horrible?

EDITH
I took your suggestion. I thought I would give Mr. Fitzgerald some advice, as you said.

Elsewhere on the stage, a tableau vivant begins to form and create the scene as EDITH describes it.

EDITH
Myself...

"EDITH" enters and poses.

Daisy's son Teddy.

"TEDDY" enters and poses.

Rather taciturn young man, you know.

"TEDDY" slumps.

And then Scott Fitzgerald.

"FITZGERALD" enters and poses.

Teddy and I got along quite well, but Mr. Fitzgerald I fear is simply unfit for public appearances.

"FITZGERALD" falls out of his pose and gulps down his cup of tea. "EDITH" turns, shocked. "FITZGERALD" sets the glass down and freezes. "EDITH" resumes her pose. "FITZGERALD" sneaks a flask from his jacket, takes a swig. "EDITH" breaks pose again to turn sharply. "FITZGERALD" freezes, slowly returns the flask, and resumes his pose. "EDITH" slowly resumes her pose. Suddenly, "FITZGERALD" rises and begins doing a raucous Charleston, knocking over the vase that GROSSIE was just seen cleaning. "EDITH" breaks her pose and covers her face in exasperation. "FITZGERALD" continues to dance as lights fade on the image.

GHOST OF JAMES
What are you working on now?

Reads over her shoulder.

A Backward Glance. You have returned to your memoir.
Yet it looks as though you are just beginning it...

EDITH
Ending it. I have been writing the memoir in reverse. The
first chapter is the last.

GHOST OF JAMES
Backward quite literally! And the reason?

EDITH
The distant past is more difficult to remember. It takes
longer to capture accurately.

GHOST OF JAMES
Hm.

EDITH
What?

GHOST OF JAMES
Is it that the past is more difficult to capture accurately or
simply to present in a tasteful, sanitized light? Only as we
get older can we be accused of making up reality...

EDITH
I have been accused of "making up" since I was a little girl.
Mother was always at her wit's end and father smiling his
secret smile - when he let me into his library it became my
own private garden. That is how I came to love books.

GHOST OF JAMES
Using them as a substitute for human contact.

EDITH
Well, at any rate Scribners is chomping at the bit for my
memoir so I really must...

GHOST OF JAMES
Scribner! He would. The old dodo. That is what they call
him, and with good reason...he shall soon be extinct! The
world is changing, Edith.

EDITH
Well, what of it? What would you have me do?

GHOST OF JAMES
Look forward! Not back...stop dealing in euphemism and
write the truth before it is too late!

EDITH
You know it is strange to hear you speak of candor since
that is the opposite of what you have always practiced.

GHOST OF JAMES
And look at me! I am a witty ghost! Do you think I like
appearing this way?

EDITH
Well if it is such a burden, then I release you.

GHOST OF JAMES
It is not that simple.

EDITH
Henry, I am at a loss. You say I am to read Fitzgerald's book.
You say I am to invite Walter on my cruise. I don't know

EDITH
Continued
what it is you want -

GHOST OF JAMES
I want you to live!

EDITH
And how will you know when I am "living?" Shall you take my pulse?

GHOST OF JAMES
I shall see it in your writing, for one -

EDITH
In my writing? My writing! All my life I have tried to capture the quality of living in my writing. Yet life is nothing like a novel. There is no structure, no build...if there is a climax, it happens early, only life lacks the keen grasp of plotting to end soon after. It goes on, and on, and on...and one is left utterly at a loss how to fill all those blank terrifying pages! Yet the older I get the more I realize what a disaster it would be if I were to capture life accurately - at least a woman's life. Do you know what my life has been? The accidents and reversals, the parade of disappointments, signifying nothing? Do you know what such a novel would be? It would convey the meaninglessness of life by being meaningless, the unbearable boredom by being boring...it would be a cerebral achievement only, a mere technical exercise...it would be a mockery of art and I would loathe it.

GHOST OF JAMES
Well it sounds like one of my later novels -

EDITH
Yes.

Beat. Softer.

Henry, has it occurred to you that perhaps there is more to
your being here than passively awaiting some epiphany on
my part? That there is something you must do as well?

GHOST OF JAMES
Of course...you are absolutely correct...

Pause.

EDITH
Well...good.

GHOST OF JAMES
Edith...I must apologize to you.

EDITH
To me?

GHOST OF JAMES
All of our correspondence through the years, the letters we
promised to burn, well - I burned, you never did -

EDITH
How did you know that I never bur -

GHOST OF JAMES
Ghost.

EDITH
Ah.

GHOST OF JAMES
I have had nothing but time to look over them again now.
Edith, some of the things I wrote you, horrible things that I
regret. Putting your writing down - discouraging you...

EDITH
Henry what on earth do you mean? No one has shown me
more support than you did. Why, it was you before anyone
else who insisted I "do the American subject. Do New
York!"

GHOST OF JAMES
Because I was doing Europe!

EDITH
Oh!

GHOST OF JAMES
I could not risk us sharing material...what if your treatment
were equal to mine? Or even worse...what if it were better?
You. A popular writer. And a woman.

EDITH
I see...

GHOST OF JAMES
I am ashamed that when I discovered your plot with
Scribner I tried to end our friendship. That my code - our
code...the same one you live by, would not allow me to
accept your kindness - to just be happy...and there is
something else, Edith. Something that I
mmm...muh...musss...

Pause. He continues, slowly and deliberately.

GHOST OF JAMES
Must tell you.

EDITH
Henry, what is it?

GHOST OF JAMES
I am afraid I have been...deviant in my passions. And I fear you will not approve.

EDITH
Approve? What on earth do you mean?

GHOST OF JAMES
It is just that in *Remembrance of Things Passed*, you were so effusive about everything but Proust's subject matter.

EDITH
Women carrying on torrid affairs with other women is beneath such talent.

GHOST OF JAMES
But my circle at Qu'acre, the young men I surrounded myself with...the artists and poets...your handsome critic Morton Fullerton....

EDITH
Well what is more natural than seeking companions of one's own intellectual stead? That is hardly "deviance" -

GHOST OF JAMES
I preferred the company of men!

EDITH
Well who doesn't?

GHOST OF JAMES
Edith -

EDITH
Furiously
Henry! I've heard enough. You say you have something to tell me, that I need to know - but I do not need to know anything because I know you! That you are the most splendid, magnificent man I ever met...and I will not tolerate anyone calling you or anything you love "unnatural," least of you - now you will stop this instant!

Edith turns away fiercely. Beat.

GHOST OF JAMES
You know, some scholars are contesting the original translation of Proust's title. That it is not "A Remembrance of Things Passed" at all.

EDITH
What is it?

GHOST OF JAMES
In Search of Lost Time.

EDITH
Considering
Yes, that is right.

Pause.

I did try, once - to write a memoir like that...the way you say. To hold nothing back. I called it *Life and I*. It is only a

EDITH
Continued
fragment now...it seems anything really true in writing or in life can only exist as fragments. And at some point you resolve yourself to nobody reading them and lock them away.

GHOST OF JAMES
Perhaps it is time to turn the key.

EDITH
It makes no difference. I am amazed at the public's density of incomprehension. It never bothered me before but now that my work draws to a close I feel it is either nothing, or far more than they know...

GHOST OF JAMES
Let them try. They may surprise you -

EDITH
They want to be scandalized Henry! Only "dirty" sells. What interest could I hold -

GHOST OF JAMES
I have read some of your fragments, Edith. "Beatrice Palmato" for instance...

EDITH
You read -

GHOST OF JAMES
Yes.

EDITH
Oh.

GHOST OF JAMES
Oh yes...

Beat.

EDITH
And what did you think?

GHOST OF JAMES
Bold. A bit sensational at times. The suspicious mother catching the daughter and father together was expertly crafted, though her descent into madness seemed a bit heavy-handed. All in all exceptionally authentic, though of course destined to remain a fragment.

EDITH
And...

GHOST OF JAMES
Yes?

EDITH
Dirty?

GHOST OF JAMES
Oh, dirty.

EDITH
Truly?

GHOST OF JAMES
Filthy my dear.

EDITH
I am gratified.

GHOST OF JAMES
It should be outlawed if it ever came to light.

Pause.

EDITH
Well, there...you see? Growing old doesn't mean one stops living. We all have strange interludes, dark secrets...why I - I...I have had an affair!

GHOST OF JAMES
With whom?

EDITH
Morton Fullerton.

GHOST OF JAMES
Ah! And I have had an affair as well.

EDITH
With whom?

GHOST OF JAMES
Morton Fullerton.

EDITH
Ohhhhhhh...

Beat. The two break into loud laughter. It goes on and on. Finally, EDITH rises.

GHOST OF JAMES
What are you doing?

EDITH
I am feeling inspired. I should like to try and finish *A Backward Glance* by nightfall. You are welcome, of course.

GHOST OF JAMES
Delighted.

EDITH types for a beat. Stops. Squints at the page.

I marvel you can see anything at all in this dim light.

EDITH
I suppose my vision is not what it once was.

GHOST OF JAMES
My dear, a girl of twenty-five would have trouble seeing in this pristine crypt.

EDITH
I suppose I could part the curtain, just a touch.

GHOST OF JAMES
Perhaps, just this once. It is beneficial to be reckless now and then.

EDITH rises. Hands on the curtain:

EDITH
Ah, Henry, what would I do without you?

GHOST OF JAMES
Without me? You never shall be! And if you should ever seem to sense it, please thus feel my arms open at their very widest, and then close about you at their very tenderest...

EDITH cracks the curtains a few inches. A beautiful ray of sunlight streams in. EDITH suddenly throws the curtains open, filling the room with light. Birds singing. It is a radiant day. As EDITH stands, bathed by the sun, GHOST OF JAMES disappears. Finally, EDITH turns, sees the room is empty.

EDITH
Goodbye, Henry.

EDITH returns to her desk and begins to work on her memoir again.

Going for a walk with her father. The episode is literally the first thing I can remember about her, and therefore I date the birth of her identity from that day...

EDITH pauses. Beat. She pushes the typewriter aside. Slowly, she reaches for a fresh sheet of paper. She then takes out an inkwell and pen. Dipping the pen in the ink, she brings it down to the page.

"Life and I..."

END OF SCENE.

SCENE THREE

The Fitzgeralds' Paris flat. The room is as littered with empty bottles of liquor as it was with paintings in the beginning of the play, the bed unmade. FITZGERALD is passed out on the floor, fully clothed. ZELDA enters tipsily, carrying the mail. She staggers her way over to FITZGERALD.

ZELDA
Mail call!

FITZGERALD
Don' wake me...first time I've slept in weeks...

ZELDA
Bill...

FITZGERALD
Oh, I'm sick -

ZELDA
Bill...

FITZGERALD
I think I'm dying -

ZELDA
Bill...

FITZGERALD
It's tuberculosis! Or a hangover...

ZELDA
Huh, now here's something.

FITZGERALD
Whazzat?

ZELDA
Letter.

ZELDA reads the address.

Edith Wharton.

FITZGERALD
Give it - to...me...

ZELDA dangles it above him. He staggers to his feet. He reads.

"Mr. Fitzgerald, touched at your sending me a copy of Gatsby - leap over previous work...congratulate you in the character of Wolfsheim on your invention of a "perfect Jew..."

ZELDA
Appalled
Oh. My. Gawd.

FITZGERALD
Shh..."present quarrel with you only this - to make Gatsby truly great ought to have given us his early career instead of a short resume - can't appreciate a character's present tragedy without intimate knowledge of his past - but you'll tell me that's the old way and consequently not your way...

Beat. FITZGERALD crumples up the letter and tosses it aside.

I need a drink.

ZELDA
The witch! The condescending old witch!

Pulls ledger from desk.

Wait, this needs to be commemorated...

She writes.

ZELDA
"March 17...Edith Wharton...witch." Hey, how do you spell "Wharton?"

FITZGERALD
Huh?

ZELDA
How - do you spell - "Wharton?"

FITZGERALD
W...A...R -

ZELDA
Oh, look, it's all your title ideas for new books..."The Skin of his Teeth," "Wore out his Welcome," "Dark Circles," "Dated..." I'm sensing a trend...

FITZGERALD sits up.

FITZGERALD
Wait, what are you reading?

ZELDA
Ooh...here's something else -

FITZGERALD
Overlapping
Hold on...

ZELDA
What's this?

Beat.

ZELDA
What the hell is this? Notes - *Tender is the Night*...Wanda,
brother, depressed, suicide after repeated nightmares of
killing mother...history of mental illness in Wanda's entire
family -

FITZGERALD
Zelda, listen -

ZELDA
Extended thoughts of patricide after Wanda is raped by her
father, age fifteen...

FITZGERALD
Wait!

FITZGERALD grabs for the ledger. ZELDA dodges.

ZELDA
Second pregnancy immediately following birth of daughter,
driven mad with guilt over decision...to abort.

Beat.

How could you do this?

FITZGERALD
They're just notes for a book I've been thinking of writing.

ZELDA
You know what they are! I'm surprised you haven't been
quoting my diary directly...like Gloria to Anthony in *The
Beautiful and Damned?* "You're so clean. You're sort of
blowy clean, like I am. There's two sorts...one's clean like
pots and pans. You and I are like streams and winds..."
Sound familiar?

FITZGERALD
Just because you have a mania for cleanliness and baths...

ZELDA
If I do it's because I feel dirty all the time now. We got dirty somehow along the way, you and me.

FITZGERALD
Zelda, every author writes from experience, writes what he knows...

ZELDA
Seems more like you write what I know to me...and what I say and write.

FITZGERALD
You don't write.

ZELDA
If I don't it's because you won't let me! What about leaving my name off the byline for all those stories we wrote together? Was that Max's idea or yours?

FITZGERALD
It's just to sell magazines Zelda. I'm the recognizable name. I still split the money with you.

ZELDA
Well maybe I'll just have to make a name for myself.

FITZGERALD
Zelda, you have a gift for language, but my strength is putting it to the page.

ZELDA
I can put it to the page too, Scott. Every time I try you say
I'm exploiting our common experiences together. Even
though every author should "write what they know" -

FITZGERALD
I'm getting tired of this.

ZELDA
Oh, right. God forbid my needs ever get addressed...out of
bed or in it.

FITZGERALD
What?

Beat.

All right, I didn't want to hurt your feelings but you know
why you're not a writer? I've shown your novel around,
everyone thinks it's too florid and erratic.

ZELDA
What about my short stories?

FITZGERALD
Your short stories are even worse! They're lopsided, they all
begin at the end! They won't sell, that's the truth.

ZELDA
I could get better, make them sell, with encouragement.
You don't want me to have my own voice.

FITZGERALD
That's not true!

ZELDA
Oh no?

ZELDA flies to a trunk at the foot of her bed and opens it.

Remember these, all my old, beautiful organdy dresses? You said they made you fall in love with me back in lil ol' backwoods Montgomery. But the second we were married you made me pack 'em away. Insisted I get new clothes in New York that made me look up-to-date...an author's wife.

ZELDA pulls some dresses out.

Lavender and pink...oooo, remember ruffles? Shall I model them for you?

ZELDA holds a dress up to her body, the dress she wore earlier in front of CAMPBELL, only not burnt yet.

FITZGERALD
Stop it.

ZELDA
Aren't you enjoying it? Then let me show you something else.

ZELDA pulls out a suit.

Remember this? The "smart suit" you bought me the day we arrived? You said it looked so sophisticated on me. Well I told you I lost it but I locked it in this trunk. I mean, if the moths can have my organdy what's a suit too?

FITZGERALD
That's enough! You can't keep behaving like this! You're making spectacles of us.

ZELDA
What? Me?

Beat.

Okay fine, I make spectacles of us. Isn't that what you
wanted? The perfect outrageous flapper wife...your "Bob-
haired bandit?" Only that's just it, isn't it? You liked it when
I flirted as long as I did it to make you happy. But the
second you suspected I did it to make myself happy, it
threatened you. You hated it. You had to destroy it.

FITZGERALD
Zelda, you cannot interfere with my career. If you ruin me,
what becomes of you? A faded debutante who was breast
fed 'til she was four -

ZELDA
I was happy in Montgomery. I didn't need you to rescue me
- my debut was the event of the season.

FITZGERALD
And you said it yourself, "what's a debut but the first time a
girl is seen drunk in public?"

ZELDA
I wouldn't go attacking others' pedigree if I were you, Scott.
"Glass houses" and all that.

FITZGERALD
I grew up on Summit Avenue, the most celebrated district
in St. Paul.

ZELDA
Yes, in the very last house on the street, just before you
turn the corner and everything becomes common again...but

ZELDA
Continued
with my writing -

FITZGERALD
You couldn't make fifty dollars on your writing. You're just a useless society woman!

ZELDA
That. Is what you want me to be.

FITZGERALD
Oh, yes! I want it! I want you to flirt with any man who comes around! I love that your affairs are practically common knowledge!

ZELDA
There's never been any affair!

FITZGERALD
Oh, just come off the roof already - everyone knows. And it's disgusting.

ZELDA
It's what I had to do. You have no confidence! You won't belong to any club that will have you! I was giving you what you needed for us to function...a chase!

FITZGERALD
Oh, so you cheated on me for my benefit.

ZELDA
Say what you want, but if I had let you know how fully you had my love and all my love, you would have walked out years ago. But you don't understand love, only money.

FITZGERALD
Oh, right! Sometimes I forget the sordid topic of coin is
below you - remind me, Zelda, when did you agree to marry
me?

ZELDA
What?

FITZGERALD
I want the date.

ZELDA
I know what you're doing and I -

FITZGERALD
When.

ZELDA
Five years ago, sometime in April, but -

FITZGERALD
It was one week after my first novel was published. For two
years I threw myself at your feet. You had my love! My soul!
I offered you all of me, and you held it at arm's length. But
the thing that got the ring on your finger was one fat
advance. So if I happen to think a woman will always care
more about what's in my pocket than what's in my heart,
then how did I get that way, Zelda? How did I get that way?

ZELDA
I waited to marry you because I knew you couldn't be happy
until you'd made a success on your own. If I had agreed to
marry you sooner you would have grown restless after the
glitter wore off and held it against me. But I'm no gold-
digger, so stop making me the enemy. We are not at war.

FITZGERALD
You say that because you think you're winning.

ZELDA
This is a marriage, Scott - there are no winners.

FITZGERALD
Oh, Zelda...truer words were never spoken.

ZELDA
Well it sounds like maybe you just hate women -

FITZGERALD
Because you are ALL - SUCH - BITCHES!

A revelation for both. Beat.

ZELDA
I have never been unfaithful to you, Scott. Not once, not in the true sense. I swear there's never been another man...

FITZGERALD
Oh, if it were only men it wouldn't be so vile! It's what people insinuate when they see you dancing with other women.

ZELDA
So it comes to this, does it? You force me to fend for myself at parties, but if I actually manage to make a friend you have to turn it into something perverted. But you will not project your own forbidden desires onto me Scott!

FITZGERALD
Just what do you mea -

ZELDA
And if I did seek extramarital fulfillment, I wouldn't exactly
be unmerited, would I? I mean it's not like you have ever
really been able to satisfy me, is it?

FITZGERALD
Maybe you are a lesbian.

ZELDA
Oh? And what about fairies, Scott? You claim to despise
them, but you're fascinated by them. What was it you used
to say? "I long to go with a young man for a paid amorous
weekend to the coast...deep calling to deep?"

FITZGERALD
It was only a goof!

ZELDA
Oh, I'm not judging you for that...but Scott, a "paid"
weekend? Do you really think you have to pay for it?

FITZGERALD
Hem was right about you...you are crazy.

ZELDA
Hemingway? Hemingway! You think I care what he says
about me?

FITZGERALD
You're just jealous.

ZELDA
Of what? A rugged-adventurer? A big game hunter,
sportsman, and professional he-man? A pansy with hair on
his chest!

FITZGERALD
Zelda! Don't say that...it's slanderous!

ZELDA
Oh really? And the time you disappeared to the bathroom
for an hour with Ernest to "compare sizes"?

FITZGERALD
It was because of you! You always try to make me feel
insufficient. I wanted his clinical opinion.

ZELDA
Really? He was just giving you his "clinical opinion" for an
hour? Well, what did he say?

FITZGERALD
He said there was nothing wrong with me, that you're crazy
and using this as a way to distract me from writing. This
and your lesbian affairs.

ZELDA
Oh, that's rich. He should put that in his next book. He can
call it "Bullfighting, Bullslinging, and Bullshi -"

FITZGERALD
Low
Zelda, please. Please. Say anything you like but lay off
Ernest.

ZELDA
La - lay off...Ernest?

Pause.

Why don't you both just sleep with each other and get it
over with? What a couple of flames!

Beat. Zelda's eyes are strange.

ZELDA
Burn it all.

FITZGERALD
What?

ZELDA
Burn it. Burn everything.

ZELDA gathers up the dresses and the suit and rushes into the bathroom.

Burn the past! Burn the future! Burn it all!

FITZGERALD
Zelda, what are you doing?

ZELDA
I'm throwing all my clothes in the tub. They need to be clean. Like the wind.

Short pause.

Now I'm striking a match.

Sound of a match being lit and a warm glow flickering from the bathroom.

FITZGERALD
Zelda? Zelda!

FITZGERALD goes to the bathroom door, which slams shut. He fights to open it.

FITZGERALD
Let me in!

FITZGERALD gets the door open. Sounds of struggle and a blow. ZELDA cries out. The sound of a tub being turned on. The fire is out. FITZGERALD emerges wringing out the suit. ZELDA appears, holding her eye. Beat.

ZELDA
I wrote you once, long ago, that we were soul-mates. But each day I feel the girl who wrote that letter slipping away. We can console ourselves with money, fame, parties - but none of it ever comes close to that first rush of love. Well some people can live like that, but not me, Scott, not me! I have to love first and live incidentally. Without that, I'll go mad, I know it! Look -

ZELDA flings the top of her blouse open. Angry red splotches cover her clavicle like the tip of an iceberg and begin to fan out as they disappear beneath the fabric.

It's been spreading for weeks...but it started here, just over my heart. You see? Do you see?

FITZGERALD gives the suit a final twist.

FITZGERALD
It's ruined, they all are...but at least the fire's out.

Beat. ZELDA covers herself. Her eyes glaze. She seems to be floating away.

ZELDA
You may have put it out this time, but we can't be on our guard forever. Everything burns eventually, and when it

ZELDA
Continued
does...that fire will consume you, and then come back for
me...

FITZGERALD
It's not as bad as all that, Zelda. It's still the Boom...

ZELDA
And all Booms end in a crash. We can leave the country but
we can't escape that, Scott. America's headed straight for it.
And when the belt is tight again there'll be nothing but time
to look back on our wasted youth.

Pause.

Oh Scott, we are America!

*FITZGERALD moves to her. She slams the door shut. Beat.
FITZGERALD picks up the ledger. He looks back at the
bathroom door. Stillness. He opens the ledger and begins to
scribble in it. END OF SCENE.*

SCENE FOUR

*Lights up on the garden outside the Pavillon Colombe.
Maybe literally presented, maybe the Garden of Eden. A
table with chairs. A small pillar with a vase on it. Voices
from inside. EDITH enters followed by CHANLER and
FITZGERALD, perhaps humming "Tea for Two."*

EDITH
You must send your dear mother my greetings, Mr. Chanler.
It seems like ages since I last saw Daisy.

CHANLER
I barely see her myself. Mother's usually too busy for me.

FITZGERALD
And Teddy here is too busy writing sad poetry to have much time for anyone, I'm afraid. This must be the first he's seen the light of day in weeks.

CHANLER looks at FITZGERALD.

EDITH
What a shame. Please be seated, both of you.

FITZGERALD flops into a chair. CHANLER sits. EDITH last, very formally. Beat.

FITZGERALD
Speaking of Daisy, I must thank you again for your letter about Gatsby. It was such a - treat.

EDITH
Of course. As I said, I thought Daisy Buchanan one of the most honest and frightening portraits of a modern woman in today's letters.

FITZGERALD
Happy to hear it!

EDITH
Except...

FITZGERALD
Except?

EDITH
Well, I am certain to your generation I must represent the literary equivalent of tufted furniture and gas chandeliers. However, if I do have a criticism I suppose it is that Daisy is too much a character, which means she is dismissable. What people need today is a violent and tragic awakening. An author who does not provide it is being remiss -

GROSSIE has entered with the tea pot.

Tea?

Pause.

FITZGERALD
Please.

CHANLER
Yes, before it gets cold. Luke warm tea is bad for my constitution.

EDITH nods. GROSSIE pours the tea and exits.

FITZGERALD
Well, I suppose you're right, Mrs. Wharton -

EDITH
Edith, please.

FITZGERALD
Edith. Gatsby could have done with another draft, I suppose - but then I guess I care more about making it new than making it perfect -

EDITH
Ah, "make it new," "make it new..." That is the current creed among you Modernists, I gather -

FITZGERALD
You should see the work it produces -

EDITH
Yes, I have read Virginia Woolf, and if you ask me *Mrs. Dalloway* is nothing but a two-hundred page excuse for not washing one's hair. By all means, make it new, but never fool yourself into believing that to be a writer's primary responsibility.

FITZGERALD
And what might that be?

EDITH
Why to make it good, Mr. Fitzgerald.

FITZGERALD
Well, it's a valid point, but these days critics seem to value innovation - even the blind sort...over quality. And you have to please critics, don't you think?

EDITH
It is when a writer attempts to do just that, Mr. Fitzgerald, that he guarantees his most disastrous reviews.

FITZGERALD
But certainly you don't know from experience?

EDITH
You would be surprised.

FITZGERALD
I had no idea. And were you...angry?

EDITH
Angry? Over a harsh review? Of course not. Why, I consider critics my collaborators. I am never angry with them. They simply surprise me sometimes.

FITZGERALD
How so?

EDITH
Well, after all, one knows one's weak points so well that it is rather bewildering to have the critics overlook them and invent others. My advice, Mr. Fitzgerald...take joy in praise as it comes, but do not make it the hook upon which your happiness hangs...you may not know what to do with yourself when you find your critics have abandoned you.

FITZGERALD
Well, to be perfectly honest it's not the critics that frighten me half so much as what the fairies will say...they're far more vicious and their vitriol isn't limited to a single column -

EDITH
Fairies?

FITZGERALD
Oh yes, I really should watch my vernacular. But you know, the fairies are everywhere and really must be taken into consideration.

EDITH
I did not know that was a term in wide, ah - circulation.

FITZGERALD
You know it?

EDITH
Walter always...that is, I have heard it used by a friend. They seem to follow him wherever he goes.

FITZGERALD
Doesn't surprise me. Really no way around 'em these days.

EDITH
And do you care for them yourself?

FITZGERALD
Oh no, not me! I can't stand fairies. Can you?

EDITH
I confess I do find them rather...taxing.

FITZGERALD
All those high-pitched voices.

EDITH
Quite.

FITZGERALD
And that inane squealing!

EDITH
Precisely!

FITZGERALD
And their pretentious little mustaches!

EDITH
Yes! And their pretentious little...ah, mustaches?

FITZGERALD
Waxed into those tiny, insufferable points, like darts...

EDITH
I'm afraid I don't follow you -

FITZGERALD
Of course, if your friend is always surrounded by fairies, I assume he is a fairy as well?

EDITH
Mr. Fitzgerald, how can a man be a fairy?

FITZGERALD
I ask myself the same question everyday Edie, I really do. Whenever I see them at a petting party or somewhere I get sick to my stomach. I knew we were two of a kind...I have a New England conscience, developed in Minnesota!

EDITH
And is that where fairies go?

FITZGERALD
Er...Minnesota?

EDITH
No, to these "petting parties."

FITZGERALD
Oh sure! You see them all the time...well, not you, per se - that is, I don't suppose you've ever been to a petting party...

EDITH
Ah, no, I'm afraid not. Although I am an avid dog enthusiast.

FITZGERALD
Oh, uh...good! That's - that's good. Everybody needs a
hobby...

Long silence.

CHANLER
Quietly
I'm allergic to dogs -

FITZGERALD
At any rate, I suppose the fairies are to be tolerated! Say
what you want, you can't sell too many books without them,
can you? And one is hardly an author without a best-seller
under his belt.

EDITH
Some would say that the true test of an author is not having
a best-seller, that it is proof of authentic literary merit to go
unappreciated by the masses.

FITZGERALD
Oh yes, I know the type well. Poor writers consoling
themselves that failure is somehow proof of their own
genius. I can't stand that type. Thank God our books sell
well and our short stories make up for it when they don't.

FITZGERALD reaches for tea.

By the way, have you got any sugar?

EDITH stares at FITZGERALD. She raises the tongs.

EDITH
One lump?

FITZGERALD
Two. I always take my tea with two lumps and a nip.

EDITH places the sugar in the cup.

Now for the nip...

FITZGERALD pulls out a flask, winks at EDITH and pours a bit of the contents into the tea. He offers the flask to EDITH. She is stunned. He offers it to CHANLER, who just looks at him. He puts it away.

Say, that's a lovely smell you get staggering up here from down the mountainside, Edie. Like honeysuckle and army leather. Must be all the soldiers loitering round the nickelodeons and brothels.

EDITH
I am - told you served in the war.

FITZGERALD
Oh sure, second lieutenant.

EDITH
That takes a noble kind of man.

FITZGERALD
I suppose it would, but I never got over.

Pause, then quickly:

It's just as well. I'd have deserted in a second given half a chance!

EDITH
You would -

FITZGERALD
It takes a certain kind of man to want to defend his country.
The man who has nothing else on his plate. Then it takes a
man like me to write about it, and a man like Chanler to put
it to music. Would you fight, Teddy?

CHANLER looks at FITZGERALD.

All right, so maybe Teddy here would fight. But that's
because he's trying to outrun the melancholia. It's in the
name you know.

EDITH
The name?

FITZGERALD
Sure. Teddy. Kind of an unstable name. No offense Chanler
my boy but it sort of just goes with crazy, you
know..naming a boy Teddy is just asking for trouble.

CHANLER looks at FITZGERALD.

What do you think, Edie?

EDITH
Mrs. Teddy Wharton.

Beat.

FITZGERALD
Of course I guess it depends on what country you were
being asked to lay your life down to protect! Maybe for
France I'd feel differently. I can see why you love it so much.
Not nearly as uptight as the states. I've got a good story to
illustrate - maybe you can figure out who it's about.

FITZGERALD rises and leans on the small pillar, almost knocking the vase off. EDITH starts. FITZGERALD broadly acts out the story while he tells it. Whenever he gets too close to the vase, EDITH starts.

FITZGERALD
A young American couple arrived in Paris from New York, he a writer and she a writer's wife. Not having a place to stay, they wandered the streets and stopped at the first hotel they saw. All went well at first, but soon the writer began to notice something strange about the hotel. There was noise and people coming and going at all hours, and the couple could not convince any of their new acquaintances to come and call. Finally, after two weeks, the writer asked the proprietor "how you expect to keep your establishment afloat if you insist on running it like a bordello!" To which the woman replied, "but sir, how should I run my establishment? It is the finest bordello in all of Paris!"

FITZGERALD bursts into laughter and slams the table while CHANLER and EDITH watch. Beat.

EDITH
Mr. Fitzgerald, I must protest. Your narrative lacks data, and you have omitted one major plot point altogether.

FITZGERALD
What? What's that?

EDITH
You have not told us what the couple did in the bordello.

FITZGERALD
Did?

EDITH
Certainly. The subject has always fascinated me...that is why
I chose to live at the Pavillon Colombe, or did you not
know?

FITZGERALD
Er, know what?

EDITH
Why, that is was a house of courtesans! Whores in your
vernacular.

*FITZGERALD is speechless. Over the next speech, EDITH
draws a cigarette out of her case. Perhaps CHANLER lights
her up.*

As soon as I heard I knew I had to have it. I find it a
constant source of inspiration in my work. I simply think of
all those women, languishing on beds in every room, and all
the strange comings and goings - ah, but now I can see that
I have shocked you. You really must excuse me. Sometimes
I forget in mixed company which topics are age appropriate.

*EDITH inhales and blows out a long stream of smoke. A
ring if she's got it. Beat. CHANLER bursts into laughter.*

FITZGERALD
What's so funny?

CHANLER
Don't you see? She beat you!

FITZGERALD
Peevish
Well, what of it?

CHANLER
In all my life I've never laughed so hard...

FITZGERALD
I'm afraid I've been ignoring you frightfully, Teddy. Why
don't we step into the library and you can tell me more of
your composing?

CHANLER
With pleasure.

EDITH rises.

EDITH
Scott, it has been lively.

She laughs.

But what did they do in the bordello?

CHANLER is gone.

Shall you stay and finish your libations outside, Mr.
Fitzgerald?

FITZGERALD
I believe I will. Such a lovely day. Far too nice to be inside
where it's...stuffy.

EDITH
I see. Well, call if you need anytime.

*EDITH passes the vase on the pillar and adjusts it to its
original position.*

FITZGERALD
My apologies for jostling it. I know how important it must
be to you that every object remain in its place.

EDITH
I believe I value consistency no more than you value
immediate gratification. My one defense is that my values
are easier on the porcelain.

FITZGERALD
You know what's the matter with you, Edie?

EDITH
No. But I've often wondered...what is it?

FITZGERALD
It's that I'll bet you've never broken anything in your life,
just for the hell of it.

EDITH
I see. And the matter with you, Mr. Fitzgerald, is that I
doubt you've ever left anything intact, just for the change of
pace. Now if you will excuse me, I shall direct Mr. Chanler
to the library. If you should chance not to be here when I
return I shall quite understand.

EDITH turns to leave.

FITZGERALD
Quickly
I didn't wan - that is...I was only trying t - I...

Pause. EDITH waits impatiently. Beat.

It's horrible isn't it?

EDITH turns back.

EDITH
Horrible?

FITZGERALD
Yes. And I suppose it's what makes a writer in the end. But isn't it horrible to be able to capture life so perfectly on the page, after the fact, but never be able to just say what you mean in the moment, when it might make a difference?

EDITH
Considering
Yes, Mr. Fitzgerald. That is...the horrible thing.

Beat.

Good afternoon.

EDITH exits. FITZGERALD stands and watches her go. He picks up his tea cup absently and brings it to his lips. Stops himself. FITZGERALD brings the cup down and stares at it. Beat. He turns and empties the cup into some plants. He sets the cup down, turns and looks at the house, then walks off in the opposite direction. The sound of footsteps fade. Long beat. EDITH reenters. Stops. Notices the cup on the table. Picks it up and sees it is empty. Scoffs. Turns to go inside. The vase on the little pillar catches her eye. She stops. Looks around. She approaches the vase. Slowly, EDITH puts her hand out, as if to tip the vase over. Hesitates. Backs away. Beat. EDITH begins to clear the tea. Behind her, title cards play and fade.

TITLE: Walter Berry did not accompany Edith on her Aegean cruise. He passed away a year later and Teddy

Wharton shortly after. Until her death in 1937, she never remarried.

TITLE: In 1940, Scott was in the midst of writing his final novel when he suffered a massive heart attack and collapsed. He was eating a chocolate bar at the time. He was 44 years old.

TITLE: Zelda spent her remaining years in and out of Highland Hospital, a mental facility.

TITLE: In 1948, a fire broke out and quickly spread to the upper floors, where Zelda was locked in the attic awaiting electroshock therapy. She and eight other women burned in the flames.

TITLE: During the Depression, Edith Wharton and F. Scott Fitzgerald fell largely out of fashion, their social novels dismissed as irrelevant as gritty political realism came increasingly into vogue.

TITLE: Today, they are considered two of the greatest - and distinctly American - authors of the 20th century.

The title cards end. EDITH enters and returns to the vase. Suddenly but decisively, she knocks the vase off the pillar. It falls and shatters. EDITH exhales and catches her breath, flushed. She is invigorated. Beat. GROSSIE enters, hearing the crash. She looks at the vase and then at EDITH.

GROSSIE
Miss?

EDITH
Clean it up.

GROSSIE
Yes, Miss.

GROSSIE kneels and reaches for the shards. EDITH watches for a moment.

EDITH
Wait...

Slowly, EDITH lowers herself to her knees until she is on the same level as GROSSIE. Edith retrieves a shard and after a moment GROSSIE opens her apron to receive it. Then another.

The women pick up the broken pieces.

END OF PLAY.

Adam Pasen's plays include *Tea with Edie and Fitz, Badfic Love, Board Fold: A Tale of Retail, Spats,* and *Starf*cker* as well as several adaptations and plays for young audiences. He is the recipient of the KCACTF National 10-Minute Play Award, the WordBRIDGE fellowship, and a BroadwayWorld Chicago Best New Play Award. He is also published in *Best American Short Plays* from Applause Books and *The Best Women's Stage Monologues and Scenes* from Smith & Kraus. His plays have received readings or productions at the Kennedy Center, Off-Broadway on Theatre Row, and in Chicago with ATC, Remy Bumppo, City Lit, and others. Finalist/Semifinalist Seven Devils Playwrights Conference and Steppenwolf Garage Rep. BA University of Illinois at Urbana-Champaign; MA Northwestern; PhD Western Michigan University with a focus in playwriting.

ALSO AVAILABLE FROM CHICAGO DRAMAWORKS

ACTION PHILOSOPHERS! by Crystal Skillman. Based on the award-winning, best-selling comic book series, witness the lives and thoughts of history's A-list brain trust leap to the stage in manic, hilarious fashion. "Totally irreverent and manically inventive!" *Publishers Weekly.* [5M, 1F]

ANYTHING AND ALWAYS... by Nic Wehrwein. The pieces of Art and Courtney's lives together are finally falling into place when Courtney succumbs to cancer. Remembering the past while turning toward the future, Art attempts to reassemble his shattered memories of Courtney while learning to live without her. [1M, 1F]

THE BEAR SUIT OF HAPPINESS by Evan Linder. In 1943, Woody, a young gay American, enlists in the army. After being shipped out to a remote Pacific Island, he is given an order: "Put up a show to entertain the men. Keep it simple. Needs music. And they like drag." Theatre of war and theatre of the mind play out together on Woody's little stage as he battles to build an identity and to be free. "This is a piece that stays with you." Chris Jones, *Chicago Tribune.* [4M]

BODIES AT REST & Other One Act Plays by Eric Peter Schwartz. Ranging from the funny to the tragic, the three original plays in this collection have two themes in common – morality and strangers. Features *Bodies at Rest, His Last Gun,* and *Pater Angelus.*

**Find scripts and licensing information for all plays at
www.ChicagoDramaworks.com**

ALSO AVAILABLE FROM CHICAGO DRAMAWORKS

CHORDS by Patricia Kane. In this one-act play, two middle-aged sisters from Tennessee reunite to record a Christmas record for their eighty year-old grandfather who raised them. Funny and touching, yet unsentimental, *Chords* explores what keeps us fighting for family when that's all it seems we have in common. [3W, 1M]

KATE AND SAM ARE NOT BREAKING UP by Joel Kim Booster. Hollywood's hottest young couple has decided to split up for good. As the media erupts in speculation and their fan base begins to dissolve, one man decides to take matters into his own hands. Kidnapped by the fan boy from hell, the pair is faced with a choice: rekindle their dead relationship or suffer the consequences. Nominated for Best New Work at the 2014 Joseph Jefferson Awards, TimeOut Chicago states, "A mixture of laughter, discomfort and heart-pounding terror. FIVE STARS!" [2M, 2F]

THE TAMING OF THE SHREW adapted by Carin Silkaitis. Hotly debated for its jaw-dropping representations of sex, gender and power, William Shakespeare's *The Taming of the Shrew* has been inspiring controversy for centuries. This gender-bending adaptation by Carin Silkaitis is set in modern Brooklyn, and asks...who's in control? Is anyone being tamed at all? [3M, 11F, 3+ ANY]

TWELFTH NIGHT OF THE LIVING DEAD by Bryan Renaud. This bloody, over-the-top comedy combines original material with text from *Twelfth Night* and *Night of the Living Dead* to explore what happens when a zombie apocalypse plagues a production of one of the bard's funniest comedies. Join the cast on stage and off as they attempt to survive - without letting the audience know what's happening! A throwback farce with surprising poignancy, *Twelfth Night of the Living Dead* puts "the show must go on" to the test. [4M, 4F]

**Find scripts and licensing information for all plays at
www.ChicagoDramaworks.com**

Made in the USA
Middletown, DE
18 May 2016